I0225230

SKANDALON:
The Study Guide

CINDY SCHROPPEL

CINDY SCHROPPEL

Skandalon: The Study Guide

Copyright © 2018 by Cindy Schroppel. All rights reserved.
Cover Design & Interior Layout: Advance Your Image, LLC

No part of this publication may be reproduced, stored in a retrieval system or transmitted in any way by any means, electronic, mechanical, photocopy, recording or otherwise without the prior permission of the author except as provided by USA copyright law.

All scripture quotations, unless otherwise indicated, are taken from the *New King James Version*®. Copyright © 1982 by Thomas Nelson, Inc. Used by permission. All rights reserved.

This novel is a work of fiction. Names, descriptions, entities, and incidents included in the story are products of the author's imagination. Any resemblance to actual persons, events, and entities is entirely coincidental.

To Contact the Author:
www.sftjm.com

DEDICATION

If it weren't for the Lord, Jesus Christ, I could not have even put pen to page. It is He who has given me such a strong desire to help others grow in their Christian faith walk. He's held onto me, strengthened me, fought for me, carried me, taught me, and I could go on and on. Without Him, I am nothing. He is the reason I live and breathe. I glorify Him and honor Him with this book.

I would also like to dedicate this book to my husband, Joe. He is my greatest supporter and has always encouraged me to use my gifts for the glory of God. He has been loving and patient with me as I've sought to grow in this journey with Christ, overcome obstacles in my life, and allowed Christ to develop His character in me. Together we have fought many battles and grown in our spiritual walk. I'm so thankful to do life with him by my side.

I also want to thank my two beautiful children, Rudy and Kalyn. They are my heart. I can't even imagine my life without them.

ACKNOWLEDGEMENTS

I would like to acknowledge my sister, Lorrie Gazette. I appreciate the time you took to review the study guide. Thank you for believing in me, sharing your thoughts, and giving your insight to make this a better study. You mean more to me than you'll ever know.

I'd also like to thank all those who've prayed for me along the way. I believe that nothing happens without prayer. Thank you.

FOREWORD

Skandalon: The Study Guide is an in-depth and practical guide. As an accompaniment to the novel, *Skandalon*, it takes the powerful principals brought forth from the book and offers sound teaching and Biblical solutions for those wanting to go deeper in their understanding of spiritual warfare. I highly recommend this study guide. You will encounter the heart of God and His desire for us to live a life of freedom and joy. It's an amazing study guide!

Fernando Ruata
Sr. Pastor of Encourager Church

TABLE OF CONTENTS

1

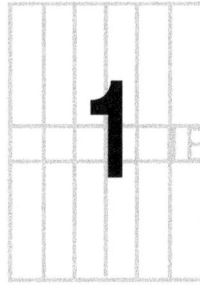

Week One Bible Study

Skandalon Reading Assignment: Chapters 1-4

Day 1

*But you have come to Mount Zion and to the city of the living God,
the heavenly Jerusalem, to an innumerable company of angels,*
Hebrews 12:22

THE MINISTRY OF ANGELS

If you were to do a search of the Bible, the word angel or angels would appear more than 250 times with at least 175 of those appearances in the New Testament. It's fair to say that angels have a strong showing in the Bible, yet we rarely hear teaching in the church regarding them.

There is a massive army that fights day and night to protect the Body of Christ against Satan's kingdom of darkness. The angelic hosts of God serve to guard, protect, guide and encourage the saints as well as bring God's judgment to the earth *(Matthew 13:49-50)*.

Angels are created beings just as humans are created beings *(Colossians 1:16)*. Their existence predates the creation of the material universe. The Bible tells us that they witnessed the creation and rejoiced over it *(Job 38:4-7)*.

Many believe that when a human dies and goes to heaven, he or she becomes an angel. Though this may prove to be comforting to some, there is no evidence in Scripture to support this belief. Scripture tells us that one day we will judge angels which indicates that we, as spiritual beings, still have a function separate from the angels *(1 Corinthians 6:3)*.

*Read **Hebrews 1**.*
There are several things we can glean about angels from this chapter.
*Look at **verse 4**. In this verse we see that Christ is _____ than the angels.*

Christ is not only much better than the angels, but *verse 6* tells us that the angels of God worship Him. They are not to be worshiped by man. Their function is to obey the voice of God and do His bidding on behalf of the Saints.

God alone deserves our worship. Christ is greater than the angels and has authority over the angels *(Psalm 103:20)*.

We are not to seek the counsel of angels but rather the wisdom of God. God may send an angel to bring instruction or direction to humans *(Acts 27:23-25)*. However, we have the Holy Spirit and the Word of God to guide us, give us wisdom and direction.

Satan can come as an angel of light. If you seek a manifestation of an angel, he'll be happy to give you one. A counterfeit that Satan uses is spirit guides. Do not allow anyone to talk you into accessing your spirit guide. It is a trap of the enemy. If you have ever allowed a spirit guide to speak to or direct you, please repent and ask the Lord to cleanse you with His blood. Bind the spirit guide and tell him he no longer has access or authority in the name of Jesus.

I knew a woman who was able to draw some of the most beautiful, seemingly spiritual pictures. However, after questioning her, I found out that she could only draw them when her spirit guide was leading her. The influence of this spirit guide kept her in a state of confusion regarding the truth of Scripture.

The only angel that we see in the Word of God receiving worship from man is the Angel of the Lord. He is believed to be Jesus Incarnate *(Exodus 3:2-6)*.

Hebrews 1:7 says, "Who makes His angels spirits and His ministers a flame of fire." The word *ministers*[1] is the Greek word *leitourgos*. From *laos*, meaning people, and *ergon*, meaning work. Therefore, the word is telling us that these angels work for the people. We see this confirmed in *Hebrews 1:14*.

Please read it and fill in the blank.
To whom are the angels sent forth to minister for? _____
_____

After forty days of fasting and being tempted in the wilderness by Satan, Christ was ministered to by the angels *(Matthew 4:11)*. They are called to assist Christ in His ministry *(Matthew 16:27)*.

Angels have great knowledge, but they are not omniscient or all-knowing *(1 Peter 1:12; Mark 13:32)*. They are very powerful, but they are not omnipotent or all-powerful like Christ. Time or space does not constrict them, but they are not omnipresent, or they can't be everywhere at one time. It is also important to note that this applies to demons as well. They are neither omniscient, omnipotent nor omnipresent. There is an innumerable company of angels.

*Read **Matthew 26:53**. How many angels are mentioned in this Scripture passage?* _____

_____

A Roman legion consisted of 6,000 men. Jesus was saying that He could have called 72,000 angels to assist Him if He'd needed their help. That means we have a mighty army at our disposal. Because they do not experience death, their numbers are not subject to decreasing *(Luke 20:36)*.

*Read **Revelation 5:8-12** and fill in the blank.*
*How many angels did John see when he was before the throne of God?*_____

_____

What were the angels doing around the throne? _____

_____

When God refers to the angels as a collective group, they are referred to as hosts *(Psalm 103:21)*. We see that Christ is head of this heavenly array.

*Read the following Scriptures: **Psalm 46:7, Isaiah 39:5, Isaiah 47:4**.*
What title is given to the Lord? _____

_____

Angels are also often referred to in Scripture as *holy ones.* *(Daniel 8:13)*
Because God is a God of order, it would make sense that there is an order or heavenly organization of the angelic beings just as there is an order of authority in the ranks of demonic beings. There is the archangel. In the book of Daniel, Michael, the archangel, is referred to as one of the *chief princes.*

> *And war broke out in heaven: Michael and his angels fought with the dragon; and the dragon and his angels fought, but they did not prevail, nor was a place found for them in heaven any longer. So the great dragon was cast out, that serpent of old, called the Devil and Satan, who deceives the whole world; he was cast to the earth, and his angels were cast out with him.*
> *Revelation 12:7-9*

Read Daniel 10:1-13.

In this passage of Scripture, we see that Daniel has been praying and fasting for twenty-one days. The prince of the kingdom of Persia (*a strong demonic presence or principality over the kingdom of Persia*) has fought to delay the answer to Daniel's prayer. Michael, the archangel intervenes so that the messenger angel can bring Daniel the answer to his prayers.

We see here that prayer and fasting greatly affected the heavenly realm. Michael was dispatched to do battle against the prince of the kingdom of Persia because Daniel was fasting and in prayer.

Gabriel is another important angel mentioned in Scripture. Many believe that he is an archangel though Scripture does not specifically mention that fact. He is believed to be God's messenger angel. He announces impending events at the will of God. He stands in the presence of God. He interprets Daniel's vision and reveals prophecy to Daniel *(Daniel 8:15-27; Daniel 9:20-27)*. He announced John the Baptist's birth *(Luke 1:1-19)*.

Read Luke 1:26-27 and fill in the blank.
Who announced the news to Mary of Christ's impending birth? _____
_____

The Bible talks about a class of angelic beings surrounding the throne of God. They are called seraphim. Their central purpose is to worship the Creator. These beings worship without ceasing. There is certainly a lesson we can learn from them.

I get so excited when the praise and worship service begins at my church. As soon as the first note echoes throughout the sanctuary, I'm on my feet and ready to get my praise on. It's my favorite part of the Sunday service. Having led worship for seventeen years, I love me some good hallelujah, shout-me-down, sing loud-and-proud kinda worship mingled in with the presence of the Holy Spirit ushering in an atmosphere of awe and wonder at the majesty and glory of God.

It fills me, sets my spirit soaring, and draws me closer to the Father. However, I can't imagine doing it twenty-four hours a day, every day! God has called us to live a life of worship. This doesn't mean that we are constantly singing songs at the top of our lungs. Though singing praise to God is an act of worship, it's not all there is to worship.

Worship is about recognizing the wonder of God in His creation, His manifested works, the sunsets and sunrises He so carefully paints, and the miraculous way He answers prayer.

*Please read **Isaiah 6:1-3** and fill in the blanks.*
In the year that King Uzziah died, I saw the Lord sitting on a _____, high and lifted up, and the train of His robe filled the temple.
Above it stood _____; each one had six _____; with two he covered his _____, with two he covered his _____, and with two he _____.
And one cried to another and said: "_____, _____, _____ is the Lord of hosts; The whole earth is full of His glory!"

The angels mentioned in this passage of Scripture are worshippers. Their entire focus is on the Lord of all Creation. I find it fascinating that even though they continually witness the majesty, might and awesome miraculous power of God, they're not desensitized to His glory. Each new display of His power propels them into a new chorus of holy, holy, holy!

I believe one of the snares of the enemy is to keep us so self-focused that we don't see the miraculous power of God that daily surrounds us. If we did, we'd be praising Him along with the angels before the throne.

The Seraphim's cry of holy, holy, holy reverberated throughout the throne room of heaven. I can only imagine that with every glimpse of the power of God, they were so overwhelmed that they could not contain their worship. It spilled forth from them like water rushing from a broken dam.

Shouldn't we respond to God in the same manner? Every time a prayer is answered, no matter how large or small...holy, holy, holy! Every time we see a miracle occur in our life or the lives of others...holy, holy, holy! The songs the sweet little birds sing so cheerfully to signal a new day should cause us to rejoice with the angels...holy, holy, holy! And, even when we are walking through difficulties and trying circumstances, does that not also demand us to worship in faith...holy, holy, holy!

*Let's close by looking up **Psalm 91:11-12**. Please fill in the blanks.*
For He shall give His _____ charge over you, to _____ you in all your ways. In their hands they shall _____ _____ _____,

lest you dash your foot against a stone.

Pray and thank the Father that His angels have charge over you today. Thank Him that they keep you and bear you up in their hands to protect you against the enemy.

Day 2

*"Likewise, I say to you, there is joy in the presence of the angels of God
over one sinner who repents." Luke 15:10*

ANGELS ON ASSIGNMENT

Read 2 Kings 6:8-17.

Elisha the prophet was a wanted man being sought by the king of Syria. Because of a prophetic revelation, Elisha was able to reveal to the king of Israel the plans of the king of Syria. The king of Syria sent an army to surround Dothan where Elisha was staying with his servant. As most of us would do upon seeing our city surrounded by a massive army, the servant panicked and cried out to Elisha. The story tells us that Elisha prayed that his servant's eyes would be opened thus allowing him to see into the spiritual realm.

*What was Elisha's prayer in **verse 17**?* _____
_____
_____

*What did his servant see (**verse 17**)?* _____
_____
_____

The horses and chariots of fire were an angelic army sent to fight against the Syrian army. There is a spiritual realm that is more real than this earthly realm we now call home. It is an eternal realm where angels and demons exist. The fact that we can't see it doesn't make it any less real. Sometimes, as He did for Elisha's servant, God will allow us a glimpse into this realm. The servant saw the angels in their chariots and horses of fire with his natural eyes. Elisha had prayed that God would open his servant's eyes because he was so full of fear. God will allow us to see into this spiritual dimension only when it is necessary to fulfill His purpose. The reason for this is that He desires us to walk by faith and not by what we can see. We must believe in faith that His angels are with us and that they faithfully guard and protect us.

> *For we walk by faith, not by sight.*
> *2 Corinthians 5:7*

*Glance back at **2 Kings 6:16** and fill in the blanks.*
So he answered, "_____ _____ _____ for those
who are _____ _____ are _____ than those who are
_____ _____."

Now, look back at Chapter 1 page 6-7 of Skandalon. We see several functions of the angels in our lives.

1. They keep a relentless vigil over us.
2. They love us and protect us.
3. They make sure that we connect with divine appointments to ensure that we are walking in the will and purpose of God.
4. They help us get back on track when we have backslidden from our faith.
5. They seek the guidance of God for their charges.

Skandalon

Ramiah would accompany her to church and observe her listening to her Sunday school teachers with a hungry heart and entering into the worship service. She would sing the praise songs at the top of her lungs, clapping her hands in perfect rhythm, and beaming from ear to ear with joy. When Zoe was ten, he was there praising, along with a host of other angels, as she made the decision to make Jesus her Savior.

It was he who had prodded her to go on the youth retreat at Pine Country when she was sixteen, which was where she'd met Michael who'd been interning as a camp counselor. He knew that it was the Almighty's plan for the two of them to meet, and he'd done everything he could to assist in the connection, making sure Zoe was in the right places at the right times.

Page 6-7

*Look at **Matthew 18:10** and fill in the blanks.*
Take heed that you do not despise one of these little ones, for I say to you that in heaven their
_____ always see the _____ of
My _____ who is in heaven.

Our angels always see the face of the Father. They take our needs to the Father and receive instruction from the Father for the ones they guard and protect. How comforting is it to know that you have angels (*plural*) that guard and protect you and are constantly talking to the Father about you?

We read in *Psalm 91* yesterday that their main assignment is to have *charge*[2] over us, to keep us, and to protect us. Not in the sense of authority, but in the sense that God has charged them to guard you and protect you.

> Who makes His angels spirits,
> His ministers a flame of fire.
> Psalm 104:4

One of the definitions of the word *charge* according to the Hebrew Lexicon, is the word command. God, the Father, is constantly giving your angels commands concerning you and your well-being.

Another word we need to look at is the word *bear*[3]. It means to carry, support, sustain, endure, aid and assist. The angels of God are always working to assist you even though you might not see them or sense their presence.

*Look at **Psalm 104:4** in the above text box.* The word *ministers*[4] used in this passage is the Hebrew word *sharat*. It means to wait on, to serve, to minister, or to attend.

*Look up **Psalm 103:20-21** and fill in the blanks.*
Bless the Lord, you His angels, Who excel in strength, _____ _____ _____ _____, Heeding the _____ _____ _____ _____. Bless the Lord, all you His hosts, You ministers of His, who do His pleasure.

In this passage, we see God's purpose for the ministry of the angels.

1. To bless the Lord in worship and service.
2. To do His Word concerning activities on earth.
3. To heed the voice of God's Word as the body of Christ confesses and declares it in the earth.
4. To minister on God's behalf for those who inherit salvation.
5. To do God's pleasure.

Angels listen to your words. They are set to flight (*to go forth to minister on your behalf*) by your words. That is why it's so important to speak and pray the Word of God. The way you get angels involved in the affairs of your life is by keeping your words in line with God's Word.

They are enforcers of God's Word to see it come to pass. We do not have the power as human beings to command angels to do anything we want them to do. They hearken to the

Word or what we speak that is in agreement with God's Word.

It is important to note that we can hinder angels from working on our behalf. Our words, spoken in doubt and unbelief and that do not agree with the Word of God can render them paralyzed from working on our behalf.

Angels long to get involved in your physical affairs – in your home, your business, your health, finances, and the salvation of your family. They open spiritual doors for you, protect you from accidents and harm, and battle dark forces on your behalf. Angels rejoice at the salvation of a lost soul.

They can bring supernatural deliverance from harmful situations *(Acts 12:5-11)*.

Angels accompany the believer into God's presence at the time of death *(Luke 16:22)*. How comforting to know that when we pass from this life to our heavenly home, we will be accompanied by our angels. We are truly never alone.

Should Christ return before we die, angels will gather God's elect to Christ at the Second Coming *(Mark 13:27)*.

There is too much to cover as to the ministry of angels. However, I would like to look at one last Scripture.

Read Hebrews 13:2 and fill in the blank.
*What warning do we receive from this Scripture?*_____
_____
_____

Angels can take on the form of man and can even consume human food *(Genesis 18:1-8)*.

The bottom line is that angels are real. They are here to help you. We are not to worship them, but we should be aware of their ministry and involvement in our lives.

Day 3

Then I heard a loud voice saying in heaven, "Now salvation, and strength, and the kingdom of our God, and the power of His Christ have come, for the accuser of our brethren, who accused them before our God day and night, has been cast down. Revelation 12:10

KNOWING OUR ENEMY

Even in the church, many do not believe in the reality of Satan. There are those who believe that he exists, yet they believe he is without power. And then there are those who believe that he exists and has limited power, but don't give much thought to his activity in the world, much less in their lives. They'd rather ignore his existence than deal with him; a dangerous choice indeed!

I've also encountered some who are so afraid of him that they refuse to mention his name as if speaking it might bring a curse upon themselves. One of the main purposes of *Skandalon* is to expose the works of Satan and his cohorts in our lives. We do not have to fear him or his power because Christ defeated him when He died on the cross for our sins. However, we are warned to be wise to his strategies and devices. Something many teachers in the church today seem to ignore.

Why are we studying about Satan? The Bible has much to say about him. This speaks to me that God would have us to be knowledgeable in regards to him. Though I don't believe that Satan is to be the constant focus of our attention or that we are to be preoccupied with him, we can't simply ignore his existence either. Some would argue that a study about the enemy only serves to give him glory. However, I believe that before going to war on a battlefield, it is always wise to know our enemy. To ensure our success in winning the war, we should want to study his strengths and weaknesses as well as his strategies and tactics.

A football coach for instance will have his team diligently study the opposing team before playing against them. They watch hours of video on their opposition where they will learn how their opponent reacts in every situation; they'll study their plays, and they'll know the strengths and weaknesses of each player in his given position.

So, our goal for the next three days is to study our enemy, gaining wisdom and understanding of our opponent! We'll discuss spiritual warfare as we dive deeper into the study in the weeks to come. But for now, I want you to have a greater knowledge of the one who stands in opposition against you.

What do you believe about Satan? How much do you know about your enemy, Satan?

_____

_____

_____

_____

_____

_____

Please read *Ezekiel 28:12-19*. In this passage, Ezekiel is speaking of an earthly king named Tyrus. However, this passage has a double meaning. It points back to the origin of Satan. We know this because Tyrus was not in the Garden of Eden nor did he walk upon God's holy mountain.

*Look at **verse 13**. How did Satan come into being?* _____

_____

Satan is not God's opposite or counterpart, nor is he in any way equal to God. Just as He fashioned man with a purpose, God fashioned or created Satan for a purpose (*He uses him like a pawn in a chess game*). The word *created* used in this passage, is the same word used in the creation account of *Genesis 1:1*. Satan was fashioned to be the worship leader of the heavenly hosts. Special timbrels and pipes were created for him on the day of his creation to make beautiful music to fill the courts of heaven. He was anointed or set apart for the service of God. He held a high office and a position of authority and walked on the mountain of God. However, God cast him out of heaven when he sinned.

If you look at *verse 12*, it says that he was full of wisdom and perfect in *beauty*[5]. This word indicates that he was perfect in his physical form. He was flawless in his beauty. It is certainly a warning to the Saints that we can be beautiful on the outside but filled with pride, arrogance, and rebellion on the inside. These are all character faults that resulted in the fall of Satan *(Ezekiel 28:17)*.

Read Genesis 3:1-7. In this account of Scripture, we see the enemy, Satan, introduced as a serpent in the passage referred to as the *fall of man*. According to the Word, he was more cunning than any beast of the field.

*In **Genesis 3:1**, what did Satan speak to Eve?* _____

_____

_____

*Now, look at **Genesis 2:16-17**. What were God's exact words to Adam and Eve?* _____
_____
_____

Satan is a deceiver and a liar *(John 8:44)*. He will come to you with a lie in hopes that you will believe it and receive it as truth instead of, and in opposition to, the Word of your God. His lies are intended to lead you astray, cause your faith to fail, and annul the purposes of God in your life. They are often mixed with just enough truth so that the hearer who is not intimately acquainted with the Word of God, will be unable to discern the difference between the truth and the lie.

Skandalon
This army of demons cowering before him took great delight in manipulating humans to do their bidding. They were a skilled army having thousands of years of experience in their trade. Their nefarious tactics had worked well for them from century to fallen century. The human heart was so utterly predictable. Anger, greed, pride, lust, envy, and jealousy, as well as a multitude of other sins, have all found their place of habitation in the heart of man since he'd first succeeded in instigating the fall of Adam and Eve in the garden of Jehovah.
Page 2

*In **Genesis 3:2-3**, how did Eve respond to the serpent?* _____
_____
_____
_____

Eve's first mistake, and one we would be wise to learn from is that she engaged the enemy in the conversation. When Satan speaks, you'd be wise to turn a deaf ear. He successfully tricked Eve into adding to and altering the Word of God. We see in our culture today, many who call themselves Christians choosing to alter God's Word to make their lifestyle choices appear acceptable to God and the Christian community. However, God's Word does not change.

*Read **Genesis 3:4**. How did the serpent respond to Eve?* _____

A common tactic of the enemy is to question the Word of God, cast doubt on its integrity and deny its veracity. Notice how he confused Eve and twisted the command of God.

It is imperative that we know the Word of God; that we read and study it, memorize it and speak it out of our mouths on a regular basis. (*Without apology, you'll hear this exhortation over and over again throughout the study!*) You can't be a part-time warrior and expect to win a full-time battle!

Read 1 Peter 5:8. Who are believers warned to be on guard against? _____

Notice that this verse refers to the devil as *our adversary*[6]. The word *adversary* in the Greek is the word *antidikos*. One of its definitions is an opponent in a court of law. Satan looks for every opportunity to accuse you to the Father. One of his greatest tactics is to make you feel condemned and guilty. He'll do all that he can to convince you that you are unworthy of the Father's love. He will set a trap for the believer hoping that we will become hopelessly snared, thus giving him an excuse to accuse us in the courts of heaven.

Read 2 Corinthians 2:10-11 and fill in the blanks.
Now whom you forgive anything, I also forgive. For if indeed I have forgiven anything, I have forgiven that one for your sakes in the presence of Christ, lest _____ should take _____ of us; for we are not _____ of his _____.

Interestingly enough, the word *devices*[7] used in this passage is the Greek word *noema*. It means a mental perception, a thought; an evil purpose; that which thinks, the mind, thoughts or purposes.

Satan's attack almost always begins in our mind. He plants a seed thought. We then must choose to receive his thought and allow the seed to take root or meditate on the truth of God's Word giving the seed no soil in which to grow.

Read 2 Corinthians 10:4-6 and fill in the blanks.
For the _____ _____ _____ _____ are not _____ but mighty in God for _____ _____ _____,

casting down arguments and every _____ _____ *that exalts itself against the knowledge of God, bringing every* _____ _____ _____ *to the obedience of Christ, and being ready to punish all disobedience when your obedience is fulfilled.*

We can stand against Satan's devices as we bring every thought into captivity. We'll go into greater depth regarding our thought life in other lessons.

Let's close this lesson with a prayer:

Father God, teach me to know my opponent and to recognize his strategies and be wise to his devices. Help me to discern when he is attacking my family and me so that I can stand against him in the name of Jesus. I ask You to begin to expose every plot and assignment against my life or the lives of my loved ones so that I can pray more effectively. I recognize that I do not have to fear him because the Greater One lives and dwells in me. In Jesus name, Amen.

Day 4

You are of God, little children, and have overcome them, because He who is in you is greater than he who is in the world. 1 John 4:4

RESISTING OUR ENEMY

Please read **1 Peter 5:8-9** *and fill in the blanks.*
Be sober, be vigilant, because your _____ *the* _____ *walks about like a roaring lion, seeking whom he may devour.* _____ *him, steadfast in the faith, knowing that the same sufferings are experienced by your brotherhood in the world.*

That word *resist*[8] is the word *anthistemi* (*think of antihistamine*). It means to set oneself against, to withstand, resist, or oppose.

When your body comes into contact with allergic triggers such as pollen, ragweed, dust mites, etc. – it produces chemicals called histamines. Histamines are the culprit behind your allergy symptoms like a runny nose and itchy eyes, sneezing, and scratchy throat. Many of us go to the store and purchase an antihistamine to combat these symptoms. The word *anti* simply means to be against or oppose. So the medicine treats the allergic symptoms by opposing or being against the histamine in our body.

We need to oppose or stand against Satan in much the same way; as he is a definite threat to the health of our body and our spiritual well-being.

Notice also that *we* are the ones called to resist the enemy. Christ dwells in and empowers every believer to stand against the attacks of Satan in our lives and the lives of those whom we love.

I used to have a serious problem with anger (*to put it lightly*). I could become enraged very easily, and it would often take me hours if not days, to overcome my anger. I hated my anger and knew that it was wrong. I was listening to a tape (*yes, it was that long ago*) of Joyce Meyer's (*my favorite Bible preacher at the time*) talking about how she'd overcome the same problem. When she would get into a fit of rage with her husband or children, she would tell the Lord she just couldn't help herself. One day, while in the midst of a fit of rage, the Lord spoke something along these lines to her, "If the Pastor were to come to your door and you were throwing one of your fits, would you stop immediately or just tell him that you could not help it?"

Because of her story, I realized that I could control my anger in front of those that I wanted to present myself to as being a sweet, mature Christian. It was my family that received the brunt of my bad behavior. I began to pray against the anger and resist the temptation of letting the anger control me. I used the Word of God and confessed it over myself. It took time, but I have overcome. I resisted the temptation to give into anger and allow it to get out of control. I withstood, and now I am free.

I still get angry from time to time, but I no longer battle the feelings of rage that plagued me for so many years, and I get past my anger quickly.

The word *resist* also implies an assertive stance against Satan's attacks. We have to be aggressive in our stand against the enemy because he is certainly aggressive in his attack against the believer. We can't resist half-heartedly. It will take time and effort on our part to resist the enemy. How long must we resist? Until the enemy flees!!!

What about you? Can you think of an area or areas that you need to resist the enemy's advance in your life? _____

_____

_____

_____

_____

_____

Write out a battle plan and include Scriptures that you could use to pray over yourself or against the enemy's schemes in your life. For instance, if you have a problem with anger, find Scriptures (Google or Biblegateway.com) that deal with anger and write them down. Pray them over yourself daily. Maybe part of your plan would be to stop and pray one of your Scriptures when you see anger rising up in you. Or perhaps you have a problem with overeating. Find Scriptures that deal with overeating and pray them each time you are tempted to overeat or eat the wrong things. _____

_____

_____

_____

_____

_____

_____

It is imperative we remember that our battle is never with our spouse, children, parents, co-workers, brothers or sisters in Christ, or any human being for that matter. The enemy will use people *(flesh)* to oppose us, but we must not fall into the trap of warring against them.

*Read **Ephesians 6:10-12**. According to this passage of Scripture, what is the body of Christ instructed to stand against?* _____

_____

Who are we not to wrestle against? _____

_____

Satan desires that we stay in strife with each other. He knows how important it is for the body of Christ to walk in love with one another. He will do all that he can to bring an occasion for offense, hurt feelings, and for bitterness or unforgiveness to take hold of our hearts.

Skandalon

"At all cost, you must keep them from walking in love with their fellow man. Utilize the weapons of accusation, offense, bitterness, and unforgiveness. It will hinder their prayer life and give you entrance to cause great havoc in their lives. Jehovah cannot bear unforgiveness."

Page 12

*Read **Matthew 4:1-11**. Who tempted Jesus in the wilderness?* _____

What three words did Jesus use each time He encountered a temptation? _____

_____

Jesus taught us a valuable lesson through this narrative. When we use the Word of God to stand against the enemy, we will always be successful in overcoming the temptations that assault us on a regular basis.

*Read **1 Thessalonians 2:17-18**. Who hindered Paul from visiting the Thessalonian church?* ___

_____

_____

We must discern who our enemy truly is, or we will waste time and energy fighting human adversaries instead of warring against the spiritual realm of darkness.

You will probably never see Satan standing beside you, pitchfork in hand, poised to attack you and destroy your life. The Word tells us that he most often presents himself to us as an angel of light. He does everything he can to make sin appear glamorous and appealing. He disguises his tactics so that they seem subtle and innocent. If we are not careful, he can ensnare us before we are even aware of it.

> *And no wonder! For Satan himself transforms himself into an angel of light.*
> *2 Corinthians 11:14*

Glance back at pages 10-14 in Chapter 1 of Skandalon. Let's look at some of the methods Satan and his demons use to ensnare us.

1. He listens to our words and uses them against us.
2. He studies our habits and our routines.
3. He attempts to get us so preoccupied with our lives that we are too busy to spend time with the Lord in prayer, study, and worship.
4. He seeks to convince us that there is more than one way to God.
5. He attempts to make us believe that we must accept the beliefs of others to be walking in the love of God.
6. He tempts us into sexual sin.
7. He attempts to confuse us as to the Biblical idea of what a family should be (a union between a man and a woman).
8. He uses mindless entertainment like television, the internet, video games, etc. to tempt us into sexual indiscretions, keeping us too busy to serve God, corrupting our morals and beliefs, and feeding lustful desires into our hearts.
9. He uses a lust for money as well as possessions, drugs, food, and alcohol to draw us away from our dependence on Christ.
10. He desires to hinder our love walk using accusation, offense, bitterness, and unforgiveness.
11. He uses fear, anxiety, and worry to diminish our faith.
12. He tries to discourage us so that we will not speak God's Word in faith over our situations.
13. He'll do whatever he can to keep us from fully understanding our covenant relationship with God.
14. One of his greatest tactics is to try and convince us that God is mad at us or doesn't love us. He wants us to believe that God has abandoned us.

Let's take a look at the Word and see what the Word has to say about our enemy and the different strategies he uses against us.

*Read **Mark 4:3-20**. Look at **verses 4 and 14-15** Who comes to take away the Word sown into the hearts of those by the wayside?* _____

_____

How soon does he come to steal the Word? _____

Be assured, the enemy of our soul wastes no time in his well thought out attacks against us. Note that in **verse 4**; the Bible refers to Satan as the *birds of the air.*

When I think of birds (*plural*), I think of a flock. I believe here the Lord is showing us that Satan has many ways in which he can steal the Word from us. He has a flock of underlings (*we'll talk about them later*) who do his bidding and are constantly working to try to wreak havoc in our lives.

Look at **verses 5-6** and **16-17**. The parable refers to seed sown on stony ground. Stony ground represents a heart that is not walking in enduring faith. Satan seeks after those who are weak in their faith so that he might steal the Word from their heart. Those who are not grounded in the Word through regular Bible reading and study will falter in their walk with God when adversity comes. Satan doesn't want you to know the Word of God because he knows that you will use it against him. He'll do everything he can to keep you from hearing, reading and studying the Word.

The word *stumble*[9] is a very important word. The Greek for this word is…(*wait for it*)… *skandalizo*! Do you recognize that word? It means to put a snare or stumbling block in the way.

Notice that it was tribulation and persecution that caused the seed to be scorched and withered. I've seen people come into a relationship with Christ with such excitement about their new-found faith, believing that from that point on life would be like a stroll in paradise. Nothing could be further from the truth. As soon as we accept Christ, we wear a proverbial target on our back.

I once knew a woman who wanted to surrender her life to Christ. She had a religious spirit as a result of being raised in a church that promoted rituals over a relationship with Christ. She was hungry and determined to know Jesus. However, her life immediately began to fall apart. Instead of applying the principals she was learning in the Word and enduring in the midst of her trial, she decided to turn away from her new-found faith and return to religion. She felt it was too difficult to stand and fight when it seemed like all hell was breaking loose in her life.

I pray that each of you studying this book will assume a fighting stance against the enemy.

You are already an overcomer.

Look at verse 7 and verse 18-19. This seed fell among thorns. *Verse 19* informs us that the thorns represent the cares of this world.

What are some of the cares listed in this Scripture?

_____

_____

_____

> *...and they have no root in themselves, and so endure only for a time. Afterward, when tribulation or persecution arises for the word's sake, immediately they stumble.*
>
> Mark 4:17

The word *cares*[10] in this verse is another interesting word. It is the Greek word *merimna.* It comes from the word *meiro,* which means to divide, and *noos,* which refers to the mind. The word denotes distractions, anxieties, burdens, and worries. It specifically addresses our anxiousness about daily life.

Do you see the picture here? Satan wants us to have a divided mind. He wants you focused on anything but the Word of God. He wants you thinking unproductive thoughts, consumed with worry and fear, and always doubting God's ability to take care of your every need.

Read 1 Peter 5:6-7. Who are we to cast all of our cares upon? _____

_____

_____

What cares have you been carrying that you need to cast upon the Lord? _____

_____

_____

_____

_____

_____

_____

Please end this lesson with a prayer. Ask God to give you a greater love for His Word and to increase your understanding of His Word as you read and hear it preached. Pray for Him to give you an abiding faith that endures through the tests and trials of life. Give your burdens, your cares, your worries and concerns over to the Lord right now. Shut the door to the enemy and don't allow him back in. Pray for the ability to resist the enemy when you are tempted to sin. Let the Word dwell richly in you.

Day 5

For if God did not spare the angels who sinned, but cast them down to hell and delivered them into chains of darkness, to be reserved for judgment… 2 Peter 2:4

SATAN'S ARMY

Before I begin today's lesson, I want to remind you that you do not have to fear Satan or his cohorts. We are studying our enemy so that we are knowledgeable as to how to win this war against him. Scripture tells us in *Isaiah 14:16* that one day we will look upon the enemy in bewilderment and say, *'Is this the man who made the earth tremble?'*

Demons are spiritual beings. God created them as angels. However, they fell when they chose to follow Satan's rebellion. We've already read that Satan, himself, was once an angel named Lucifer *(Isaiah 14:12-14)*. The name Lucifer means *light bearer*. He was created to bear the light of Christ. He was created beautiful and full of wisdom. He was anointed and perfect in all of his ways until the sin of pride was found in him. He desired to be like the Most High. He sought to exalt himself above God.

Skandalon

There was a time he'd loved and served the great Jehovah. He'd seen His power displayed in creation both of the physical world and the humans who occupied it. He, along with the holy angels, had rejoiced over the great wonder of it all. But Jehovah's demands for reverence and such single-minded worship proved to be more than he could bear. Jehovah could not, or would not, share His throne with anyone else, and it sickened Beelzebub to the core.

Jehovah himself had proclaimed that Beelzebub was the anointed Cherub. His resplendent beauty was matchless…except to One. All of the holy angels had been aware of his position and power. He'd led the heavenly choir in such majestic worship, hitting musical notes the likes no human ear has ever heard or even imagined, and no celestial being could match. That should have made him worthy of worship too. He'd convinced at least a third of the angels to bow down in worship to him. They'd recognized his giftedness and were in awe of his beauty. They were ready to give him the homage he felt he too deserved. He'd convinced them that one day they would rule and reign with him for all eternity.

Page 2

*Please read **Ephesians 6:12**. This list serves to help us understand Satan's hierarchy. Please list them below.*

_____   _____

_____   _____

Satan has a highly organized kingdom. His demons have different assignments as well as different territories. Much like the order of the angels of God, Satan's army has those of differing ranks and authority. Incapable of anything new, he's simply copied what God set in motion from the beginning.

Principalities and powers appear to be the highest levels of Satan's hierarchy. Though the Bible doesn't go into detail, we can gather from Scripture that their assignment is most likely to protect the enemy's territory in countries and regions of this world. The Greek word for *principalities*[11] is *arche* therefore it may refer to fallen archangels. The word *arche* means beginning or origin. These created beings existed at the beginning of all things.

It is Satan's purpose to deceive the nations, bring forth war and destruction among the nations, and keep the lost from obtaining a knowledge of God's truth and salvation through His Son Jesus Christ. He uses these demonic beings to assist him in his mission.

We see an example of a principality in *Daniel 10:10-13*.

Please read the passage and answer the questions below.
In this passage, we see that an angel was sent to prophesy to Daniel but he was held up by a principality. Who withstood the angel? _____
For how long did he withstand the angel? _____

_____

You'll notice that it took Michael, one of the chief princes (*angels*) to help battle this principality indicating that this was a very powerful being.

*Please read **Ephesians 1:15-23**. Now please look back at **verses 20** and **21** and fill in the blanks.*
…which He worked in Christ when He raised Him from the dead and seated Him at His right hand in the heavenly _____, far above all _____ and power and might and dominion, and every name that is named, not only in this age but also in that which is to come.

Jesus is seated far above all principalities. These principalities must bow down to His authority. However, on earth, we are the ones who are to carry out His authority doing battle in the heavenly places through spiritual warfare. (*Note: It is not wise to stand alone against a principality unless you are well trained in spiritual warfare, have been given specific authority by God, or are under a spiritual intercessor who has been given authority to pray over a specific principality.*)

> *And from the days of John the Baptist until now the kingdom of heaven suffers violence, and the violent take it by force.*
> Matthew 11:12

Look at Ephesians 2:5-6 and fill in the blanks.
And raised us up _____, and made _____ sit together in the heavenly _____ in Christ Jesus.

We have a position of authority over the enemy. Though we must use wisdom in spiritual warfare, we are not to cower or run in fear when he attacks us or those we love. We are to take our seated position next to Christ and take authority through spiritual warfare over the enemy.

The word *powers[12]*, found in *Ephesians 6:12*, is used to describe another position in Satan's hierarchy. It is the Greek word *exousia*. Let's look at some of its meanings so that we might have a deeper understanding of our enemy: physical and mental power; the ability or strength with which one has been endued, which he either possesses or exercises. Including the power of authority or influence and right (*privilege*), as well as the power of rule or government. These powers refer to those set in a position of power over Satan's kingdom of darkness. It's important to remember that the only power they have over us as believers is what we give to them.

Read Colossians 2:15 and fill in the blanks.
Having disarmed _____ and _____,
He made a public spectacle of them, triumphing over them in it.

Through the power of His cross, Christ has triumphed over our enemy. The enemy's power is limited to that which we allow him to have in our lives. We are assured victory against the enemy's attacks when we stand and fight using the Word of God, the name of Jesus, and the blood of Christ.

Scripture also mentions the rulers of the darkness of this age and spiritual host of wickedness operating in our world system. The Bible is not specific as to their function. However, we can assume they have specific areas or assignments in which they oversee.

These are a host (*army*) of demons who carry out Satan's orders and assignments against individuals, ministries, churches, etc. Their purpose is to destroy the kingdom of God by whatever means necessary.

Let's look at the Word and see some of the workings of these demons.

*Read **Luke 7:21**. In this Scripture, what do we see demons referred to as?* _____
_____
_____

*Read **Mark 5:1-15**. What type of behavior did the demons incite in this man?*_____
_____
_____
_____

*What does this passage tell us as to the name of the demon and what did the name mean (see **verse 9**)?* _____
_____

*Read **Mark 9:14-29**. What type of spirit was attacking the boy?* _____

*What would happen when the spirit seized the boy (see **verse 18 and 22**)?* _____
_____
_____
_____

*Read **Matthew 12:22**. This demon-possessed man was healed of what ailments?*_____
_____
_____

Remember, Satan does not stand on your shoulder in a red suit with horns on his head and a pitchfork in his hand. His attacks are subtle and often unrecognizable.

I want to close this lesson with a very powerful reminder from *Revelations 12:11*:

*And they overcame him by the **blood of the Lamb** and by the **word of their testimony**, and they did not love their lives to the death.*

2

Week Two Bible Study

Skandalon Reading Assignment: Chapters 5-8

Day 1

"O my dove, in the clefts of the rock, in the secret places of the cliff, let me see your face, let me hear your voice; for your voice is sweet, and your face is lovely." Song of Solomon 2:14

HEARING THE VOICE OF GOD

I can't tell you how many times I have heard Christians say, *"I never hear from God."* If you are a child of God, you hear His voice. The question is not *if* you can hear His voice; it's a matter of determining the manner in which He most often speaks to you. During this week's lessons, we'll discuss the multitude of ways in which the Lord speaks to us. I'm hoping that you will discover His still small voice within the pages of these lessons. But, I also pray that you will realize that He speaks to you daily. He speaks to you intentionally. He speaks to you intimately. He speaks as a friend, a teacher, as one who corrects and guides, and as a comforter. He speaks provision and faith to your deepest need. To pain and loneliness, He speaks hope and peace. He speaks grace and mercy when you fall short. He speaks calming words to ease your fear in the midst of the storms of this life. His great passion is to commune with you.

Read Isaiah 50:4-5b. Fill in the following blanks.
He _____ me morning by morning, He _____ my ear to _____ as the learned.

God understands our need to hear His voice because He shares the same desire towards us. He longs to hear our voice. When we became born again by the Spirit of God, our spiritual ears were awakened to hear His voice, much like a radio tuned to our favorite station. Each new day holds the promise of intimate communication with our beloved Lord. The number one key to hearing the voice of God is to be absolutely convinced that He not only desires to speak to you but also that He *is* speaking to you.

Read Jeremiah 33:3 and fill in the blanks.
God says that if we will call upon Him, He will _____
What does He promise to show those who call upon Him? _____
_____

Read Psalm 91:15 and fill in the blanks.
He shall _____ _____ _____ *, and I* _____
_____ *him.*

His promise is that *if* we call upon Him, He *will* answer!

The word *call*[13] is the Hebrew word *qara*. It means to call out to someone; cry out; to address someone; to shout, speak out, or to proclaim. It carries the meaning of crying out to someone to gain their attention.

I have three precious grandchildren who hold a very large portion of my heart. I can promise you that when they desire to gain my attention, all they have to do is say, "*Nanny.*" Bam…there I am, at their side and ready to answer them or take care of their need. I don't always give them what they want, and my answer isn't always what they are hoping to hear (*though I have been accused of giving them cookies for breakfast just because they asked for them*). However, I don't ignore them. When they call, they always receive an answer from Nanny.

God loves us far more than the love I have for my precious grandchildren. Therefore, when you call…He answers. You may not perceive His answer if you don't comprehend the ways in which He speaks.

It is the glory of God to conceal a matter, but the glory of kings is to search out a matter.
Proverbs 25:2.

As a child, I can remember playing outside on a hot summer day with my friends. One of our favorite games to play was hide-and-seek (*Yes, we really did play outside even though the thermometer often approached 100 degrees in the Texas heat. We didn't have video games, computers, Facebook or iPhones.*). I'm sure you are familiar with that game. So is God. He loves to be the One who hides and thoroughly enjoys being chased and sought after by you.

I can remember back to the early days of my walk when I was maturing in my relationship with the Lord. Just as soon as I thought I had figured out how He chose to communicate with me, much to my dismay, He'd begin speaking in another manner so that I would chase after Him once again.

Often, I found myself wondering if I was able to hear His voice or if I had sinned or offended Him in some way causing Him to cease talking to me. It was confusing, to say the least. However, it would drive me to seek after Him like a desert wanderer searching for the next oasis.

Read Proverbs 8:17 and fill in the blanks.
I love those who love me, and those who seek me _____*will find me.*

God has the answer to every question you can think to ask and the wisdom and revelation for every need in your life. However, He's looking for those who will diligently commune with Him. Hungry hearts receive answers. We must seek Him continually and consistently until we receive the answer.

Read James 1:5. What does this Scripture tell you about God's willingness to answer your questions?
_____
_____

According to the Greek Lexicon, the word *wisdom*[14] refers to intelligence, or knowledge of matters that concern your life. It refers to things of human nature as well as the divine. It can mean the interpreting of dreams and visions. It pertains to wisdom in the management of the affairs of life and the proper way to approach the unsaved, as well as the understanding of Biblical truths.

In essence, God desires to give you wisdom in every area of your life. To gain this wisdom, all you have to do is seek Him.

Read Isaiah 30:21 and fill in the blanks.
Your _____ _____ _____ *a word behind you, saying, "This is the way, walk in it," Whenever you turn to the right hand or whenever you turn to the left.*

God can speak in several ways. The most common way that He speaks to His children is through His Word. He can also speak through a dream or vision. We see in the story

Skandalon

In the dream, he'd looked into her crib and reached to cover her with her blanket. He remembered thinking how innocent she looked and sensed the need to protect her. He'd turned to get something…maybe another blanket to cover her or perhaps her pacifier…He couldn't remember…but when he turned back to the crib; she was gone.

Pages 19

of *Skandalon* that Michael has a warning dream in which God was trying to prepare Him for a future event.

Read the following Scriptures and then match them with the description as to how God speaks to His children.

Acts 22:7-8	*He speaks prophetically, through our circumstances or our senses*
Acts 12:7	*We may hear His audible voice as if He were standing next to us speaking plainly and with great authority*
Exodus 3:4	*He places a song in our heart that conveys a message or a point He's trying to make*
Psalm 42:8	*People can convey a message from God to His children*
Hebrews 1:1	*He may use an angel, if necessary*

There will be seasons in all of our lives when it seems as though we can't hear from God at all. I've experienced this many times. I refer to it as a desert or wilderness season. It is a time in our walk when our faith is being tested. In this season, we have to draw deeply from the wells of our salvation. We must learn to trust that Jesus is true to His Word and that He will never leave us or forsake us. It is a time where we must take steps of faith based on the truth of His Word and trust that He is guiding us. If we allow the Lord to have His way in our life, we will be drawn into greater intimacy with Him during these seasons.

> Then He said, "Go out, and stand on the mountain before the Lord." And behold, the Lord passed by, and a great and strong wind tore into the mountains and broke the rocks in pieces before the Lord, but the Lord was not in the wind; and after the wind an earthquake, but the Lord was not in the earthquake; and after the earthquake a fire, but the Lord was not in the fire; and after the fire a still small voice.
>
> *1 Kings 19:11-12*

The important thing to remember during this time of testing is that He loves you and is with you.

*Look up **Jeremiah 29:13** and fill in the blanks.*

And you will _____ Me and _____ Me, when you _____ for Me with all your heart.

Stop and think about the last time you know you heard or discerned the voice of God. Write down the method He used to speak to you and the message you received from Him._____

_____

_____

_____

_____

_____

If you couldn't remember a time, don't worry. I believe that by the end of this week, you will hear and recognize the voice of your Father. Pray this prayer with me:

*Father God, I long to hear Your voice above all other voices. Open my eyes to see You and my ears to hear You. Speak to me in my night season through dreams and visions. Help me to discern when you are speaking to me through my circumstances. I believe that You speak, and I can hear Your voice according to Your Word in **John 10:27**. I thank You for knowledge, understanding and for clarity. In the name of Jesus. Amen.*

Day 2

Give ear and hear my voice, listen and hear my speech. Isaiah 28:23

EARS TO HEAR

Considering the Bible as our source and the fact that the King James Version has approximately 788,280 words (https://www.biblebelievers.com), I believe it's safe to assume that God likes to speak (*He created women, didn't He?*). So, if He enjoys talking to His children, why is it that even those of us who understand how He speaks, often can't hear or discern His voice? We are in a relationship with a living God. He desires to be close and intimate with each one of us. So let's go deeper in our walk with Him and learn to hear His voice, even if He chooses to speak in the gentlest of whispers.

When speaking to the seven churches in the book of Revelation, God always gave them a warning. *Please read the following verses: Revelation 2:7; Revelation 2:11; Revelation 2:17; Revelation 2:29; Revelation 3:6; Revelation 3:13 and Revelation 3:22.*

Write down the recurring warning given to each church: _____
_____
_____

How does this warning speak directly to you? _____
_____
_____
_____

If God warns the church that we must have ears to hear, we can assume that He knows there are times in our life when our ears are not tuned in to His voice. In these technological times we live in, most of us have experienced the frustration of losing our signal while talking on our cell phone. The person on the other line is speaking, but we can't comprehend what they are saying because the signal is weak or diminished altogether. Usually, when the signal is gone, we lose contact with the person with whom we were conversing. It can be very annoying, to say the least. Likewise, our ability to hear from the Lord can become weak, or we can lose the ability altogether. Let's look at a few reasons as to why we may not be perceiving the voice of our Father.

Please read and write down **John 10:27.** _____
_____
_____
_____

If you are His sheep, you can and should hear His voice. One hindrance to hearing the voice of God is doubt and unbelief that He is Who He says He is and that He'll do what He says He will do. We can't please God when we are not willing to believe His Word. We must believe that He desires to reward (*speak to*) those who diligently seek Him.

God spoke to Abraham and told him that He would make his descendants as numerous as the stars in the heavens *(Genesis 15:1-6)*. Abraham was well over seventy-five years old, and his wife was barren when He heard the Lord's voice speak faith promises to him. In order to see such a humanly impossible promise come to pass, he had to make a firm decision to believe that God was speaking to Him and that He would be faithful to do what He promised.

> *But without faith it is impossible to please Him, for he who comes to God must believe that He is, and that He is a rewarder of those who diligently seek Him.*
>
> *Hebrews 11:6*

Please read **James 1:5-8** *and fill in the blanks.*
If any of you lacks _____, *let him* _____*of God, who gives to* _____ *liberally and without reproach, and* _____ _____
_____ _____ _____ _____. *But let him* _____
_____ _____, *with no doubting, for he who doubts is like a wave of the sea driven and tossed by the wind. For let not that man suppose that he* _____ _____
_____*from the Lord; he is a double-minded man, unstable in all his ways.*

To hear the voice of God, you must have a firm belief that when you ask, He will be faithful to answer you. He is pleased when you seek Him for wisdom, direction, understanding, etc. He has promised to direct and guide you throughout your journey here on this earth *(Proverbs 3:5-6)*.

The word *doubting*[15] in this verse carries the meaning of having a conflict within oneself. It renders the idea of hesitating or having misgivings, having a divided heart when making decisions or wavering between hope and fear.

Satan knows that if he can get you to doubt that you've heard from God on any one issue, you'll constantly be in doubt as to whether or not you can discern God's voice.

My prayer for you is that from this moment forward, you will be confidently assured that you can and will hear the voice of your Heavenly Father speaking to you.

Read Matthew 7:7-12. How does this Scripture convey God's willingness to speak to you? ____

_____

_____

_____

_____

The concept of asking, seeking and knocking tells us that we are to continue to bombard heaven until our answer comes. Often, we fail to receive the answer because we give up while it is on its way to us. We have to remember that God's timing is not the same as our timing but His promise to us is to work everything together for our good in His time *(Ecclesiastes 3:11)*.

Read Matthew 13:10-17. Look back at verse 11 and fill in the blank.
*He answered and said to them, "Because*_____

_____,

but to them it has not been given.

We must have a teachable spirit to hear from heaven. If we are not teachable, the Holy Spirit cannot bring correction or instruction when needed. We often believe that we know the truth based on what man has taught us. However, if our truth doesn't line up with the Word of God, it is not truth but mere teachings and interpretations of man. We need to be like the Bereans and search the Scriptures daily to find out if what we hear from those preaching and teaching is the absolute truth *(Acts 17:10-15)*.

Read John 15:1-8. In verse 7, what is the promise given to those who abide?

_____

_____

_____

Certainly, a key component to hearing the voice of God is to abide in His presence. To *abide* connotes an active, living, constant intimacy with Christ. You can't attend church on Sunday morning and then forget about seeking Him as you go about the rest of your week expecting to have a fulfilling relationship with Christ.

If you want to hear God's voice, you have to seek His presence regularly but not religiously. I have a prayer time almost every day. Usually, it's in the morning as soon as I wake up and make myself a cup of coffee (*I'm praying that there will be coffee in heaven*). I like to spend about an hour reading my Bible and praying. Up until just a few years ago, if I missed my prayer time or failed to spend what I deemed to be the proper amount of time in His presence, I would assume God was disappointed in me. I also believed the lie that I couldn't and shouldn't expect His favor in my life or His anointing on my ministry if I wasn't spending quality time with Him every single day. This deception led me to seek Him out of a performance-based, religious mentality. However, I've since learned that my relationship with God is much deeper than a one-hour prayer session. A greater understanding of His grace has assured me that if I can only spend twenty minutes with Him, it can be just as deep and fulfilling for both of us. I've learned to seek Him because I love Him, enjoy, and find fulfillment in His presence whereas I used to seek Him because I'd feel guilty and condemned if I didn't (*a very common ploy of the enemy*).

I've also learned that it's possible to seek Him throughout my day. I try to stay aware of His presence and listen for His voice. I seek His advice regularly, and I thank Him immediately when I sense Him speaking to me. I include Him in the large and small moments of my day.

The point I'm trying to make is that our relationship with the Lord isn't about time constraints, it's about intimacy. We build intimacy by spending quality time abiding with the Lord throughout our day; thanking Him and praising Him as we witness Him working in and through our lives. We'll talk more about this in our lesson on prayer.

Skandalon

Zoe laid on the edge of her side of the bed as if the touch of her husband might contaminate her. Because of His great love and mercy, the Holy Spirit whispered into her spirit. "For if you forgive men their trespasses, your heavenly Father will also forgive you. But if you do not forgive men their trespasses, neither will your Father forgive your trespasses."

However, as in times past, she chose to reject His voice and hold on to her pride and anger. She rolled over with her back to Michael and tossed and turned until she fell into a fitful sleep.

Page 41

Read James 1:19 and fill in the blanks.
So then, my beloved brethren, let every man be _____ to hear,
_____ to speak, slow to _____ .

We must learn to become swift to hear the voice of our Shepherd so that we can be quick to obey. Otherwise, we can open ourselves up to the enemy, believing the lies he whispers into our souls. The more I learn to tune into the Good Shepherd's voice, the better I will be at discerning the difference between the truth and a lie.

Something to think about: *Describe your relationship with the Lord? Do you feel like you have a relationship with Him that is deep and abiding or is it more of a shallow relationship? Do you think your relationship with the Lord could be more fulfilling? What are some steps you can take to make sure that you are spending quality time with Him? _____*

_____
_____
_____
_____
_____
_____
_____
_____
_____
_____
_____
_____
_____

Day 3

Behold, I stand at the door and knock. If anyone hears My voice and opens the door, I will come in to him and dine with him, and he with Me. Revelation 3:20

HINDRANCES TO HEARING

Jesus often spoke kingdom truths in parables or stories. The religious leaders of the day and those who followed after them, could not understand or comprehend these truths *(Luke 8:10)*. We can also miss the voice of God if we choose a religious lifestyle *(righteousness achieved by doing good works)* over an abiding walk with Christ *(righteousness paid for by His death on the cross for our sins)*.

God is looking for intimacy with His children. You cannot achieve intimacy by merely following a religious system of rules and regulations. Jesus gave a great analogy of how our relationship with Him should be, through the picture of a shepherd and his sheep *(John 10:1-30)*.

Sheep follow the shepherd because they've experienced his goodness, his protection, and his love. They know their shepherd looks out for their best interest. We should follow Christ out of a love-filled heart for Him; a grateful heart that understands how very much He loves us in return.

When we consistently sin or are living a lifestyle that is in direct opposition to God's Word, it can hinder us from hearing the voice of God.

*Read **Hebrews 10:19-23**. Look back and **verse 22** and fill in the blanks.*
Let us _____ _____ with a true heart in full _____
of faith, having our hearts sprinkled from an _____ conscience and our bodies
washed with pure water.

When we have unrepentant sin in our lives, we open the door for guilt, shame, and condemnation to speak to us. Their voices can be so deafening that it becomes difficult to hear the voice of our Good Shepherd. We need to be quick to repent and turn away from sin. When our conscience is clean, we find that we can enter into His presence with ease. Please understand this fact; the Lord never abandons us. He waits with open arms for His children to run into His presence. When we are living in sin, we tend to hide from Him because shame deceives us with the lie that God is angry and therefore, He does not want to commune with us.

Read James 4:7-10. Please write out the promise of God to you in James 4:8 in the blanks below: __
_____
_____

God promises us that if we draw near to Him, He will draw near to us. However, when we draw near to God, it must not be with a double-minded heart. Our hearts must be set on listening for His voice, obeying His Word and following His will for our lives.

If we are seeking after the world and the things of this world, we will drown out His still small voice.

Unforgiveness, bitterness, and anger will keep us from having ears to hear. We'll talk more about this in a future lesson.

A stubborn and a rebellious heart, as well as an unteachable spirit, can cause us to listen to only what we want to hear and believe. Thus, hindering us from hearing and receiving what God desires to speak to us.

> *"Be angry, and do not sin": do not let the sun go down on your wrath, nor give place to the devil. Let him who stole steal no longer, but rather let him labor, working with his hands what is good, that he may have something to give him who has need. Let no corrupt word proceed out of your mouth, but what is good for necessary edification, that it may impart grace to the hearers. And do not grieve the Holy Spirit of God, by whom you were sealed for the day of redemption. Let all bitterness, wrath, anger, clamor, and evil speaking be put away from you, with all malice. And be kind to one another, tenderhearted, forgiving one another, even as God in Christ forgave you.*
>
> *Ephesians 4:26-32*

Please take the time to read Isaiah 30:1-10. It's a bit lengthy but very important in making this point. Please fill in the following blanks.
Refer to verse 1: "Woe to the rebellious children," says the Lord, "Who _____
_____ *but* _____ _____ _____."

Often we can't hear or discern the voice of God because we run to the world for answers before we think to run to the One who holds the world in His hands. How many times do we pick up the phone and seek out a family member or a friend's advice before we've sought the Lord in prayer about a matter?

Refer to **verse 2**: *"Who walk to go down to _____, and have not _____ _____ _____, to strengthen _____ in the strength of _____."*

A psychic will never give you the answers you seek. Psychics are merely pawns, used of the enemy to deceive you. The internet is full of wisdom, but the wisdom that it offers does not compare to the wisdom of God. The many religions of the world may make those who follow them feel better. However, these religions offer a false security and superficial wisdom.

In the above references, Egypt is symbolic of the world. We must seek first the kingdom of God if we want the wisdom of God in all matters concerning us.

Skandalon

Michael enjoyed and even looked forward to his study and prayer time with God every day. Nothing could compare to the times when God would speak and make His presence real. He loved when the word came alive, and he received nuggets of revelation as he studied. On several occasions, he'd heard God's audible voice, which drove him to seek Him that much more. However, he knew that he'd slipped in his spiritual walk, and was not happy as he reflected on some of the ways he'd allowed the world to creep into their home. Television shows that had once been considered off-limits from watching due to the language, sex scenes, and violence were now recorded if there was a possibility they might miss them. He and Zoe rarely prayed together anymore. When they were dating, they had made it their habit to pray together on the phone before hanging up each night. Life kept them both so busy that it had somehow crowded out what had once been so important to them. And then there was the debt, which kept him filled with anxiety every month when the bills were due. It was the cause of the knot in his stomach and the oppression he was experiencing this morning.

Page 9

Refer to **verse 9 and 10**: *That this is a _____ people, lying children, children _____.*
Who say to the seers, "_____ _____ _____," and to the prophets, "Do not prophesy _____ _____ _____ _____.
Speak to us _____ _____, prophesy deceits.

I don't know about you, but I think that's some scary stuff. We may not have used those exact words, but how many of us have said the same thing in our hearts? We must desire God's truth above all else even when we know it might not be what we want to hear. I can promise this; a word of correction from God is far greater than never hearing His voice at all. God will never speak anything to us that would bring forth pain without purpose.

We have to guard against our emotions getting in the way of hearing the truth as well as our desire to have our own way. It is always in our best interest to pray the words found in the Lord's Prayer:

Your kingdom come. Your will be done on earth as it is in heaven. **Matthew 6:10**
What about you, have you ever ignored or disregarded something the Lord spoke to you because it wasn't the answer you wanted to hear? If so, what was the outcome of the situation? _____
_____

Busyness will hinder you from hearing God's voice. There are times when we need to learn the discipline of being still.

I once was seeking God while on the way to minister at a women's retreat. I had been seeking Him for an answer to a need in my life but hadn't heard from Him though I had prayed intently about it. The Lord gave me a vision of a bunch of bees buzzing around me. When I asked Him what the bees represented, He told me *"busyness."*

If it's been awhile since you have heard His voice, consider the fact that you might simply be too busy. Ask the Lord what you might need to cut out of your schedule so that you can hear from Him. Nothing you cut out of your busy life is more important or valuable than hearing from heaven.

There are times when we cannot hear from the Lord because we haven't obeyed or acted upon the last thing He told us to do. If you haven't heard His voice recently – think back to the last thing He spoke to you. Did you pay attention? Did you obey?

Are you asking God to give you dreams and visions but are frustrated because you don't seem to be able to hear from God in this manner? Did you take the time to seek Him for the meaning of the last dream He gave you?

*Write down the last thing God spoke to you. Did you act on it? Meditate on it? Search His heart regarding it?*_____
_____

How did you respond to or acknowledge His voice? _____
_____

Take a moment to pray and ask God to help you be quick to obey when you hear His voice. Ask Him to continue to point out anything that would hinder you from having ears to hear what He has to say to you. Make sure that you praise Him and thank Him for His sweet fellowship!

Day 4

The Mighty One, God the Lord, has spoken and called the earth from the rising of the sun to its going down. Psalm 50:1

HOW DOES GOD SPEAK

Jesus is the living Word of God. Therefore, I think it's very safe to say that the number one way God speaks to us is through His written Word. For this reason, it is so very important that we read, study and memorize the Word on a regular basis.

*Read **John 1:1-2** and fill in the blanks.*
In the _____ was the _____, and the _____
was with God, and the _____ was God. _____ was in the
beginning with God.

Skandalon

Taking a seat after worship was over, he was startled as his eye caught the scripture on the cover of the Sunday bulletin. It was the same scripture in Isaiah the Lord had quickened to him the day before in his quiet time.

When you pass through the waters, I will be with you; and through the rivers, they shall not overflow you. When you walk through the fire, you shall not be burned, nor shall the flame scorch you.

Isaiah 43:2

Michael didn't hear a word of the sermon. The scripture kept whirling over and over in his mind as he tried to figure out what God was speaking to him. Maybe He was trying to warn me about the anger and resentment I'm feeling today. He thought about how disappointed he was in Zoe and himself for his ungodly attitude. Ashamed that he hadn't even tried to fight against his emotions or cast down negative thoughts, he left church feeling defeated instead of encouraged. Certain that God was disappointed in him, he didn't even bother asking for His help.

Pages 27-28

When I was a young woman, living alone in an apartment without a phone (*BC – before cell phones*) or a roommate…I had a man try to break into my apartment. He kept wriggling my doorknob and banging on my door. Did I mention that I was alone without a phone? I was so terrified that I grabbed a can of Easy-Off Oven Cleaner and a butcher knife and sat by the door all night long.

In the midst of this terrifying moment, the Lord brought a Scripture to my remembrance that I'd learned in Vacation Bible School as a small child. It was *Psalm 56:3, Whenever I am afraid, I will trust in You.*

I wasn't even walking with the Lord at the time, but I knew He had reminded me of the Scripture. I repeated it over and over again until I finally fell asleep. That Scripture was life-giving and brought peace when I was so desperately afraid. I've never forgotten that incident.

Did you catch how He spoke to me? He just reminded me of a Scripture that had been deeply embedded in my spirit since childhood. The Word had to be in me for Him to speak it to me.

He can speak to us as we read the Word or bring a Scripture to our remembrance when we need it. He can also speak to you when you hear the Word being preached. We often refer to this as a Scripture being quickened or magnified to us. Have you ever been reading your Bible when a Scripture passage seems to jump off the page at you? This is the Lord quickening a Scripture to your spirit.

*Read **Matthew 4:4** and fill in the blanks.*
But He answered and said, "It is written, 'Man shall not _____ by bread alone, but by every _____ that proceeds from the _____ of God.'"

*Read **1 Thessalonians 2:13** and fill in the blanks.*
For this reason we also thank God without ceasing, because when you _____ the _____ of God which you _____ from us, you welcomed it not as the word of _____, but as it is in truth, the word of _____, which also effectively _____ in you who believe.

The Word of God can change your outlook on life, transform your situation, bring you peace, comfort, and direction. It can bring healing to the body, soul, and spirit. When God speaks His Word to you, it can elevate you to new spiritual heights and transform the way you think. It can even birth life into dead situations.

No matter how God speaks to you, what He speaks will never go against His Word. It is the measuring rod for determining the difference between God's voice, your flesh and the voice of the enemy.

Another manner that God uses to speak to us is through the counsel of spiritual friends and leaders. Though we may seek the counsel of a brother or sister in the faith, we must always be sure that their words of wisdom line up with the Word of God.

Read **Proverbs 24:6** and fill in the blanks.
For by _____ _____ you will wage your own war, and in a _____ _____ _____ there is safety.

In *Skandalon*, we see this illustrated through Michael seeking the counsel of his friend, father, and pastor. God also used people to speak into Zoe's life.

Read *Acts 21:10-11* and fill in the blank.
Who did God use to speak to Paul? _____

He can speak to you through radio, television, a sermon, a teacher…and the person doesn't even have to be a Christian. He spoke through a donkey to the rebellious prophet Balaam **(Numbers 22:22-35).**

God will use His creation, natural objects or circumstances to speak a spiritual message to you. God once used a rotted tree that had fallen in a friend's neighborhood to speak prophetically to me about a situation. The fallen tree represented something that God

> …but he was rebuked for his iniquity: a dumb donkey speaking with a man's voice restrained the madness of the prophet.
> 2 Peter 2:16

was declaring to be dead in my life. It was an answer to prayer for wisdom and direction regarding a relationship.

Read **Psalm 19:1-4** and fill in the blanks.
The heavens _____ the glory of God; and the firmament _____ His handiwork. Day unto day _____ speech, and night unto night _____ knowledge. There is no speech nor language where their voice is not _____. Their line has gone out through all the earth, and their _____ to the end of the world.

Read **Matthew 21:18-22** and fill in the blanks.
What natural object did Jesus use to convey a spiritual truth to the disciples? _____

_____

What was the spiritual point He was trying to make? _____

_____

_____

_____

God speaks through the inner voice of His Spirit dwelling within us. Sometimes His voice can be audible and sometimes His voice is simply a spontaneous flow of thoughts. Generally speaking, it's something you know you didn't or wouldn't think of on your own.

His audible voice is unmistakable.

Read 1 Samuel 3:1-20. It's a bit lengthy, but I want you to be encouraged that if God can and will speak to a child, He will certainly speak to you.

Did Samuel perceive that it was the Lord speaking to him at first? _____

Who did he think was calling his name? _____

Did Samuel hear the voice of the Lord in his spirit or was it audible? _____

When you hear the audible voice of God, it sounds just as if He were standing beside you speaking. When He speaks to us in an audible voice, it is because what He speaks is very important and something that must be acted upon immediately.

God has spoken to me audibly. However, those times are rare. Once, while at a friend's birthday party, God asked me to pray for a woman who was attending the party. He told me that I was to pray for her to get pregnant. I didn't even know if she wanted to get pregnant, so I argued with Him. Though no one else was aware of our conversation, He was very persistent and even shouted at me until I obeyed. Three months after the party, she announced that she was pregnant.

He speaks to us Spirit to spirit. The Holy Spirit speaks directly to our spirit. It is sensed as a spontaneous thought, idea, word, feeling or a picture that suddenly pops into your mind or is impressed upon you. Often, you will mistake it for being your own thought.

Again, it's most important to remember that what He speaks will always agree with His Word. God will never instruct you to do anything that goes against His Word.

God often speaks to me through a song. I might wake up with a song in my heart. Or, I might hear a song on the radio and the words to that song minister to my need. Pay attention to the songs that run through your mind. I try to listen to Christian music, so my spirit is edified by the words of the songs.

I will never forget the time God spoke to me through a Rod Stewart song (*go figure*). For a season in my life, I would sing, "*Have I told you lately that I love you*" to the Lord at the end of our prayer time together. One day, while out shopping with my daughter, the Holy Spirit stopped me and told me to "listen." My daughter was in the dressing room trying on clothes, and I was rummaging through a rack of undergarments. When I stopped to listen, I heard *our song* playing over the music system in the store. It brought tears to my eyes because I knew He was singing it back to me.

Has God ever used music to speak to you? If so, write down the song and how it ministered to you. __
_____
_____
_____
_____
_____
_____

*Have you ever heard the audible voice of God? Do you remember what He spoke to you?*_____
_____
_____
_____

Day 5

Then He said, "Hear now My words: if there is a prophet among you, I, the Lord, make Myself known to him in a vision; I speak to him in a dream. Numbers 12:6

GOD SPEAKS THROUGH DREAMS AND VISIONS

Spiritual dreams and visions are another way in which God can speak to His children. Many today miss out on an opportunity to hear from the Lord because they do not believe that God still speaks to men in dreams. I find this form of communication from God to be most exciting. I often equate it to a riddle or puzzle that must be solved. However, it keeps me constantly seeking Him until I receive the interpretation.

Read Job 33:14-16 and fill in the blanks.
For God may _____ in one way, or in _____. Yet man does not _____ _____. In a _____, in a _____ of the night, when_____ _____falls upon men, while slumbering on their beds. Then He _____ the ears of men, and _____ _____ _____.

'And it shall come to pass in the last days, says God, that I will pour out of My Spirit on all flesh; Your sons and your daughters shall prophesy, your young men shall see visions, Your old men shall dream dreams. And on My menservants and on My maidservants I will pour out My Spirit in those days; and they shall prophesy.
Acts 2:17-18

Read Acts 2:17-18 in the above text box. In this familiar passage of Scripture, God makes it clear that He still speaks through dreams and visions. He used dreams to speak in the Old Testament as well as the New Testament. Dreams were instrumental in the lives of Old Testament prophets as well as in the life of Joseph, the earthly father of Jesus, and also in the life of Paul, and many others.

Most people simply dismiss dreams. Some say they never dream while others do not believe that God would speak through a dream. There are several books on dreams and dream interpretation that I highly recommend. One of my personal favorites is *Understanding the Dreams You Dream*, by Ira Milligan. However, we must remember that God is the true interpreter of dreams and visions. If you seek Him, He will give you the interpretation.

The more you pay attention to your dreams and write them down, the more understanding God will give to you. Most of the symbolism God uses in dreams will be familiar to you. God will also use symbolism from the Word. I encourage people to keep a dream journal. In my dream journal, I often write down the dream as well as anything that I might have been praying about or that is going on in my life to which the dream might pertain.

Dreams can be speaking about present situations in your life, or they can be prophetic, meaning they speak of future events. They can bring comfort, guidance or correction. God will use color, symbols, people, and emotions to speak to you in dreams. He may also give you words of knowledge, words of wisdom, or prophecy for others through dreams.

Another important point to make about dreams and visions is that you have to be careful of the mindset in which you try to interpret them. For instance, I used to have a spirit of condemnation ministering to me. So, therefore, I interpreted almost everything the Lord spoke to me as a message of conviction or rebuke instead of receiving love and instruction from Him.

You can often manipulate the interpretation to be what you think or want it to be if you are not in submission to God or familiar with His voice.

I do not believe that all dreams are from God so you must learn to determine the source of your dream. *Jeremiah 23:32* speaks of prophets who prophesied false dreams. Some dreams are simply the result of our soul being cleansed and working through the struggles and turmoil going on in our lives.

> "Behold, I am against those who prophesy false dreams," says the Lord, "and tell them, and cause My people to err by their lies and by their recklessness. Yet I did not send them or command them; therefore they shall not profit this people at all," says the Lord.
> Jeremiah 23:32

Again, search for good Christian books on dreams and dream interpretation.

Usually, a God-given dream will be one that you remember as soon as you awaken from sleep and often, God will awaken you so that you remember it. Sometimes, when I'm having my prayer time, God will remind me of a dream I had during the night. There are also times that I might see something that triggers the memory of a dream. When this occurs, I believe that the dream is from God, and I will seek Him regarding its meaning.

Why would God speak to us in dreams? We can be so busy with our minds racing so much of the time that it's difficult for us to hear the voice of God. However, when we are sleeping, our mind is at rest and able to receive from God in a dream.

Surely I have calmed and quieted my soul, Like a weaned child with his mother;
Like a weaned child is my soul within me. Psalm 131:2

It's so important that our soul is quiet and calm to receive what the Lord would speak to us. Obviously, for some of us, this is very difficult. Especially for type A personalities like myself, whose minds go a mile a minute the moment our feet hit the floor. Therefore, God can speak to us in dreams and visions when we are still rested from sleep or in the midst of our sleep.

If you have a recurring dream, it is most likely because God is trying to convey something important to you, and you are not understanding or comprehending His message.

Satan can also influence your dreams. There are ways to determine the source of the dream. Any dreams that come from Satan will not line up with the Word or the nature of God. They will not bring peace. Usually, a dream that comes from the enemy will bring confusion. It will bring fear and accusation. Remember, Satan is the accuser of the body of Christ.

The best way to discern the giver of the dream is to know The Giver of dreams personally. The more you get to know the Lord, the more you will be able to discern His voice above your own or that of the enemy.

*Read **Habakkuk 2:1** and fill in the blanks.*
I will stand my watch and set myself on the rampart, and _____ to _____ what He will _____ _____ _____. And what I will answer when am corrected.

Sometimes we listen for God to speak. However, at other times we must watch for what He will say.

Visions are like dreams only the recipient is awake. A vision can be a picture that pops into your mind, or it can seem like a mini movie playing in your mind. Again, God is the interpreter, and when you seek Him, if the message is from Him, He will give you revelation.

There are times that the Lord may give you a picture of another person. More likely than not, it is because He desires for you to intercede for that person. Usually, that person will be someone that is very close to you. However, I have experienced times when it is a person I've never met, yet I know He is calling me to pray at that moment for a complete stranger.

God most often speaks to me with pictures. I might see a picture or vision in my mind. It is up to me to seek Him as to the meaning or interpretation of the picture. If He gives me a word of knowledge for another person, it is most often by this method. As I begin to share what I am seeing with the other person, I will usually get the interpretation of the picture.

It is important to understand that God will speak a word to you for someone else's edification and encouragement. Therefore, you must discern if a message from the Lord is for you or someone else. I once had a dream that was so vivid. When I awoke from the dream, I thought it was a word for me. But as I sought the Lord in prayer, He showed me that the dream was a word for my best friend. It turned out to be a powerful prophetic word that she desperately needed.

Read Acts 10. Again, this is a long passage, but you can see how God gave Peter a powerful vision that resulted in the salvation of Gentile converts.

Often God will give you a vision upon waking. It's because your mind is at a place of rest and ready to receive.

Skandalon

Grandma Abby was suddenly awakened from a deep sleep at three-thirty in the morning. She sensed the presence of God in the room. "What is it, Lord?" she asked. Her granddaughter's face came to her mind. She felt a strong urgency to get up and pray for Zoe. She quickly obeyed. Wiping the sleep out of her eyes, she grabbed for her glasses on the bedside table. She went into her living room, sat down in her favorite chair, and prayed for about an hour until she felt the peace of God come upon her. Assured her prayers had been effective and that God was pleased, she went back to bed.

Page 42-43

Read **Psalm 46:10** *and fill in the blanks.*
_____ _____, *and know that I am God; I will be* _____
among the nations, I will be _____ *in the earth!*

When we get still so that we might hear and receive from God, He is exalted in our life.

We have to remove or get away from the distractions like the television, radio, phone, etc. for a time so that our ears are prepared to hear.

Worship is a great way to get your mind to focus on God instead of your daily list of things to do. Often, before going to sleep at night, I will spend some time in prayer and worship to prepare my spirit to receive from the Lord during the night season.

When in prayer, write down anything that comes to mind that you need to accomplish during the next day so that you can forget about it and keep your mind focused on the Lord.

Can you remember a time when God has spoken to you in a dream or vision? What was the purpose of the dream or vision? Was it for you or a message for someone else? _____

_____

_____

_____

_____

_____

_____

Get still before the Lord and ask Him to speak to you. Listen for His voice but also watch for Him to speak through a picture or vision. Write down what He says to you. _____

_____

_____

_____

_____

_____

_____

3

Week Three Bible Study

Skandalon Reading assignment: Chapters 9-12

Day 1

You number my wanderings; Put my tears into Your bottle; Are they not in Your book?
Psalm 56:8

WHY IS THIS HAPPENING TO ME???

"Why is this happening to me?" This is a common question often asked when all hell is breaking loose in our lives. When bad things happen, even though we believe that we are doing everything right, or when the unexpected event creeps into our space, we can be tempted to question God's motives.

> *Or do you despise the riches of His goodness, forbearance, and longsuffering, not knowing that the goodness of God leads you to repentance?*
> *Romans 2:4*

Many would believe the lie that God is behind all of their negative circumstances including sickness and disease so that He might teach them a lesson or somehow get glory out of their situation. The Word tells us that it is God's goodness that leads us to repentance. He loves us and wants the best for us. As we've said before, He'll use negative circumstances to receive glory as we overcome our trials and difficulties. However, He's not an unmerciful, unkind God and He does not put sickness on one of His children to force obedience.

Let's get one thing straight right off the bat...God is not the author of the bad things that happen in our lives. Jesus gave us an example of how the Father thinks and acts on behalf of the believer. He always went about doing good while He walked this earth. His soul desire was to obey the will of the Father.

The world would like to blame God for all the terrible things that occur, and certainly, the enemy would like to cast doubt on the goodness of God. However, God is good, and He desires good things for your life. Does that mean that you should never have to experience difficulties? No!

*Please read **John 16:33** and fill in the blanks.*
These things I have spoken to you, that in Me you may have _____.
In the _____ *you will have* _____;
but be of good cheer, I have _____ *the world."*

The word *tribulation*[16] comes from a Greek word *thlipsis*. In Biblical times, the juice of the grape or olive was produced by means of crushing or pressure under heavy stone slabs. *Thlipsis* is the word used to describe this process. The word speaks of pressure, stress, anguish, adversity, affliction, crushing, squashing, squeezing and distress. It also denotes a narrow place that causes one to be hemmed in. Can we all relate?

We have all been through seasons in our lives of intense crushing. Though God may not be the one to cause this intense pressure, He will use it to bring about the most precious oil in our lives.

Skandalon
What have I done? I've served Him all of my life."
"Michael, I wish I had all the answers. I know God's plan for our life is always perfect, even when it doesn't appear to be just or fair. I know He is working out His plan for you and Zoe. Sometimes we have to go through the storm before we can see the rainbow. Like Joseph in the Bible, you might have to go to the pit before you get to dwell in the palace. God's promise to you is that He knows the plans He has for you. You have to have faith that His plan is for your ultimate good. You only see a part of what's going on, but God sees the big picture from start to finish. And though it may take all that is in you right now, you're going to have to trust Him."

Page 128

*I know most of us know this next verse of Scripture, but please look up **Romans 8:28** and fill in the blanks.*
And we know that _____ _____ work together for _____
to those who are _____ according to His purpose.

God will take everything you and I walk through or experience, both good and bad, and use it for His good purpose in our lives. He is not the one who is responsible for all of the bad things that occur, but He will certainly receive glory in the finished product of our lives. Can I get an, Amen?

It's very natural to question God as to why we are experiencing difficult situations or seasons in our lives. However, we must come to the place of trusting Him to work out every trial for our good. He never wastes anything and uses all of our life experiences to mold and shape us into the man or woman of God He has called us to be.

I was molested very early on in my childhood by several men. One of the men was my grandfather. I know what it means to go through difficult times. I still bear the emotional scars of this molestation. However, God has given me numerous opportunities to use the pain that occurred in my childhood to bring comfort and understanding to others.

He didn't ask me to call the molestation that occurred in my life *good*. But He did take the bad things that happened to me and use them for His glory. I wish I could say to you that I never questioned God as to *why* they happened. I did! I wish I could say that I don't look back in regret that they happened. Of course, I do. However, I can say that they are an integral part of my makeup. These horrific incidents from my childhood have helped mold and shape me into the woman I am today. God uses the oil that was created through these crushing times to anoint the lives of others.

I've never experienced the unimaginable loss of a child or my spouse though I've known the loss of a father. I know that nothing compares to the loss of a child, having witnessed this incredible pain through the eyes of my sister and my best friend. Their walk through the valley of the shadow of death was difficult to watch. All I could do was pray for them and be there as much as possible when they needed and reached out for support. However, I do know that God has been a constant in their lives. He's met them in their pain and disappointment, walked with them down lonely roads, held their hands and caught their tears in His nail-scarred hands. The Father is very cognizant of the pain incurred through the loss of a loved one, and He grieves with you. He lost His own Son. If you have walked, or are still walking in the midst of this valley, please know that He is with you and will never leave you.

*Please read **2 Corinthians 1:3-4** and fill in the blanks.*
Blessed be the God and Father of our Lord Jesus Christ, the Father of mercies and God of all _____, who _____ us in all our _____, that we may be able to _____ those who are in any _____, with the _____ with which we ourselves are _____ by God.

I have seen God take from the seemingly most unredeemable situations in life and use them as a means to bring comfort and encouragement to others. He can do the same in your life if you'll allow Him the opportunity.

Though I've seen my sister and my best friend go through different stages of grief, I've also watched them bravely entrust each new day to God. They've decided to trust when they could not see, believe when they couldn't understand, and hope when all hope appeared to be lost. They've put one foot in front of the other, took one step at a time, cast their hands into the hands of Jesus and have overcome by the blood of the Lamb. But their healing began when they entrusted their pain to Him.

*Read **1 Thessalonians 4:13-14** and fill in the blanks.*
But I do not want you to be _____, brethren, concerning those who have _____ _____, lest you _____ as others who have no _____. For if we believe that Jesus died and rose again, even so God will bring with Him those who sleep in Jesus.

*Please read **1 Peter 1:1-9**.*

> *"O Death, where is your sting?*
> *O Hades, where is your victory?"*
> *1 Corinthians 15:55*

Verse 3 speaks of a living hope. We have this living hope because Christ suffered death for us, taking away the pain and sting of death. We do not have to grieve as those in the world without hope because we know that death is not the end for the child of God. For the born-again believer, it is the beginning of our eternal existence. We have the promise that we will see our loved ones again if they made the decision to follow after Christ while on this earth.

But we also have this living hope while experiencing difficulties on this earth. It is the hope that Christ can and will redeem every negative situation in our lives.

We have all experienced terrible pain, loss, and trials to some degree. However, when the unexpected happens, and we've searched the heart of God as to *why* and there seems to be no other answer…it may simply be because we live in a world where sin, sickness, and disease just happens.

*Please read **Romans 5** (Yes, all of it!) and fill in the blanks.*
Verse 12: Therefore, just as through _____ _____ sin entered the world, and _____ through sin, and thus _____ spread to _____ _____, because all sinned.

Because Adam fell, sin entered this world, and death came through that sin. Sometimes, the only reason as to why we experience trials and tribulations in this world is because we live in a fallen world where sin abounds more and more. No other explanation! But keep reading because Christ came to bring good news!

Verse 17: For if by the one man's _____ death reigned through the one, _____ _____ those who receive _____ of _____ and of the gift of righteousness will _____ in life through the One, Jesus Christ.

I want you to note that you have an abundance of grace to reign in life as you walk through every trial and negative circumstance. God's grace will carry you through and see to it that you overcome. We can rejoice in the hope that Christ will reign victorious over every negative circumstance in our life. Because we are loved and adored by Jesus, our hope will not be in vain *(verse 2-5)*.

Before we close out this lesson, I want you to see that your pain is not in vain.

*Look at **Romans 5:1-5** and fill in the blanks.*
Verses 3-5: And not only that, but we also glory in _____, knowing that _____ produces _____; and _____, character; and _____, _____. Now _____ does not disappoint, because the _____ of God has been _____ _____ in our hearts by the Holy Spirit who was given to us.

God doesn't waste a thing. Every tear is carefully captured in a bottle and recorded for His glory. Your pain will work for you an incomprehensible treasure. Let's close out today with one last Scripture.

*Read **Romans 8:18-25**. Fill in the blanks.*
Verse 18: For I consider that the _____ *of this* _____
time are not worthy to be compared with the _____ *which shall be*
revealed in us.

Verse 20-21: For the creation was subjected to _____, *not*
_____, *but because of Him who subjected it in* _____;
because the creation itself also will be _____ *from the bondage of*
_____ *into the glorious liberty of the children of God.*

There is a far greater glory that outweighs any sufferings we might experience while on this earth. God has placed hope in each of our hearts. It is a hope for that which we cannot see with our natural eyes yet; it is more real than the earth beneath our feet.

We may not necessarily be able to explain away our pain. However, we can put our hope in His ability to carry us until we have worked through the pain.

Can you think of a time when God has redeemed your difficult circumstances? How did He bring beauty for ashes? How has He used your trial to encourage others? _____
_____
_____
_____
_____

Day 2

But in my adversity they rejoiced and gathered together; attackers gathered against me, and I did not know it; they tore at me and did not cease; Psalm 35:15

I Think I'm Under an Attack!

No one in the body of Christ is exempt from an attack of the enemy. As a matter of fact, one glance through the Word will reveal to you that you are in very good company if you have been or are currently under attack. Jesus, John the Baptist, the Apostle Paul, just to name a few, were some whom we read suffered attacks by Satan and his demons.

If you are a believer, you have a real enemy who hates you with a passion.

*Read **Revelation 12:12**. According to this Scripture, why is Satan filled with wrath toward the believer?* _____

Satan has many schemes and strategies in which he uses to attack the believer. But the point or purpose of his attack against you is to keep you focused on what he is doing so that he can distract you from the purposes of God for your life.

He'll do all that he can to get you so focused on the length and strength of your trial that you forget how incredibly great and awesome your God is. He desires that you would fear his ability to curse you instead of being assured of God's ability to bless you.

Our focus should always be on God's love for us, His ability to bless, protect and keep us from every attack of the enemy. Don't get caught up in the attempt of the enemy to distract and discourage you.

Have you ever heard the saying, "*Don't look at how big your mountain is, look at how big your God is?*" When we focus on how impossible our situation is, we take our eyes off of our God, Who is well able to do the impossible on our behalf.

> *Therefore we also, since we are surrounded by so great a cloud of witnesses, let us lay aside every weight, and the sin which so easily ensnares us, and let us run with endurance the race that is set before us, looking unto Jesus, the author and finisher of our faith, who for the joy that was set before Him endured the cross, despising the shame, and has sat down at the right hand of the throne of God. For consider Him who endured such hostility from sinners against Himself, lest you become weary and discouraged in your souls.*
>
> *Hebrews 12:1-3*

As soon as we recognize that we are under an attack of the enemy, our attention should turn to the Word of God that can counter the enemy's schemes aimed strategically against us.

*Read **1 John 4:18** and fill in the blanks.*
There is no _____ in_____; but _____ _____ casts out _____, because fear involves torment. But he who _____ has not been made perfect in _____.

When we are experiencing an attack of the enemy, no matter what form it comes in, we can become fearful if we are not rooted in our understanding of the Father's love for us. One of the greatest weapons we have to counter an enemy attack is the knowledge that we are supremely, richly, and infinitely loved by the Father. Hopefully, by the end of this Bible study, we will know His love to a whole new measure.

*Read **Job 1:1-12**. Look at **verse 1** and fill in the blanks.*
There was a man in the land of Uz, whose name was Job; and that man was _____ _____ _____ and one who _____ God and _____ evil.

According to this passage of Scripture, we could assume that Job wasn't doing anything to provoke such tragic loss in his life. By looking at his wealth and the possessions he had accumulated as well as the number of children he had, we'd call him a blessed and highly favored man of God. Even though he was a godly man, he still went through a season of tremendous suffering in his life.

Many in the church mistakenly think that if someone is experiencing a trial, they must be doing something wrong. They have grave sin in their life, or even, perhaps, they've been knocked to their knees by God because of pride. There is no evidence in this passage of Scripture that states Job was doing anything wrong. God declared in His Word that Job was blameless and upright.

*Look at **verse 6**. The sons of God here refer to the angels who'd come to present themselves before the Lord.*
Who came among the sons of God? _____
_____
_____

*Look at **verse 7**. And the Lord said to Satan, "From where do you come?".*

Please record Satan's answer.

_____

_____

_____

In this Scripture, we see Satan's territory is on this earth that we dwell upon. His appearance before the throne is to cause destruction to God's kingdom and to accuse the body of Christ.

This passage also teaches us that Satan is accountable to God. He cannot attack you or me without the express consent of God. Why would God allow an attack against a believer, you might ask?

> *Many are the afflictions of the righteous, but the Lord delivers him out of them all.*
> *Psalm 34:19*

*For a possible answer, please read **James 1:2-3** and fill in the blank.*
My brethren, count it all joy when you fall into various _____, knowing that the _____ of your faith produces _____.

Spiritual growth comes through trials. We are forewarned that we will have trials and tribulations as long as we are in this world. But we are also encouraged in Scripture that Christ has overcome the world.

Trials are meant to make us lean into the Father, and grow in our trust of His love and care for us. They also strengthen our faith. They show us how much we have grown in our relationship with the Lord. Like a light shining into the dark areas of our heart, they magnify areas in our walk that are weak and in need of strengthening.

Skandalon

"Zoe." Michael's voice was tender as he knelt down beside her, reaching out to comfort her. Her body stiffened at his touch. "Baby, I don't know why He didn't intervene. But I know His love for us never fails. I know He's promised to comfort and carry us through this. We have to trust Him. Remember the story of Job in the Bible? Even though he lost everything, he still trusted God. In the end, he saw the goodness of God. That's the God I choose to continue to believe in."

Page 80

You've heard it said that you couldn't have a testimony without a test, and you can't have a rainbow without a storm. Trials give us our testimony and bring out the proverbial rainbows in our lives. At the end of a trying season, we experience the faithfulness of our God.

Read *Job 1:8* and fill in the blank.
Then the Lord said to Satan, "Have you _____ *My servant Job, that there is* _____ _____ _____ *on the earth, a* _____ *and* _____ *man, one who* _____ *God and shuns evil?"*

Notice that God was bragging, if you will, on His servant. God knew how strong Job was, but He wanted to demonstrate to Satan that His servant would not fail nor succumb to his evil schemes. Satan wanted to disprove Job's faithfulness. God wanted to prove the sincerity of Job's faith.

This trial was a statement of God's faith in Job to come through the fire of testing purified as gold. He has the same confidence in you and me.

If you've never read the book of Job, I encourage you to read this book in its entirety. In the end, you'll discover that God restored Job's losses and gave Job twice as much as he'd had before his trial began. *(Job 42:10)*

Read *Luke 22:31-32* and fill in the blanks.
And the Lord said, "Simon, Simon! Indeed, _____ *has* _____ *for you, that he may* _____ _____ _____ _____ *. But I have prayed for you, that your* _____ *should not* _____*; and when you have returned to Me, strengthen your brethren."*

Peter was handpicked to be a disciple of Jesus by the Father. Peter had spent hours in the presence of the Lord. We see that he, like Job, was attacked by the enemy with the permission of the Father.

Peter was to be instrumental in the foundational building of the Church. The Father had to be sure that his faith was strong, that he was a man of integrity and rooted in his love for Christ as well as His people. He also desired that Peter would come to grasp the unfathomable grace that would be offered to him after denying Christ. In His sovereignty, God chose to allow a temptation at the hands of the enemy to purify Peter.

The word *sift*[17] used in the above passage speaks of an inward agitation to try one's faith to the verge of overthrow. In other words, to press one until they feel they can be pressed no more. It also refers to the sifting process that occurs when wheat is shaken in a sieve. This process separates the impure from the pure.

Let's look at one last Scripture. Please read **Luke 4:1-2** *and fill in the blanks.*
Then Jesus, being _____ _____ _____ _____
_____, returned from the Jordan and was led by the _____
into the _____, being _____ for forty days by the
_____. And in those days He ate nothing, and afterward, when they had ended,
He was hungry.

Who led Jesus into the wilderness to be tempted by the enemy? _____

You may be going through one of the most difficult trials of your life. Please, understand that God is still in control. He has His hand on your life and is well able to stay the enemy when he has overstepped his bounds.

Rest in the Father's love for you today. Trust that He can see you through every trial and negative circumstance. Be of good cheer, for He has overcome the world!

Day 3

If you do well, will you not be accepted? And if you do not do well, sin lies at the door. And its desire is for you, but you should rule over it." Genesis 4:7

DOORS WIDE OPEN

> Be angry, and do not sin.
> Meditate within your heart on
> your bed, and be still. Selah
> Psalm 4:4

There are times in our lives when *we* give entrance to the enemy. We open a door, so to speak, for him to come in and wreak destruction. To keep unwelcome intruders from our home, what do we do? We keep our doors locked. We carefully guard who we allow in. Spiritual doors work in the very same way. We keep unwanted spiritual intruders out by closing and locking the door.

*Read **Ephesians 4:26-27**. Fill in the blanks.*
"Be angry, and do not sin": do not let the sun go down on your wrath, nor give _____ to the _____.

According to the Greek Lexicon, the definition of the word *place*[18] is a portion or space marked off. It can mean an inhabited place or an occasion for acting. We can let Satan into our place and give him an opportunity to act up in our lives. We can give him a space that becomes his marked-off territory. A scary thought indeed!

We learn from this passage, one of the ways in which we give him an open door is by holding onto anger. God understands the human heart better than we understand it ourselves. He knows that there are times when we will become angry. Interestingly enough, He doesn't tell us never to become angry. He warns us not to sin in our anger. So, the question would be, how do we sin in our anger? I firmly believe the answer to that question can be found in *Ephesians 4:31-32*.

Please read the Scripture and fill in the blanks.
Let all _____, _____, anger, clamor, and _____ _____ be put away from you, with all _____. And be kind to one another, tenderhearted, _____ one another, even as God in Christ forgave you.

72

We see in this passage that bitterness, wrath, anger, clamor (*loud quarreling*) and evil speaking are all lumped together. Anger that is out of control can lead to a bitterness of the soul and cause damage in the life of the believer. If we are not careful, anger can take over our life.

*Read **Hebrews 12:14-15** and fill in the blanks.*
Pursue _____ with all people, and holiness, without which no one will see the Lord: looking carefully lest anyone _____ _____ of the grace of God; lest any root of _____ springing up cause trouble, and by this many become defiled.

Anger can quickly turn into bitterness. Bitterness defiles the soul just as cancer eats away at the body. I've heard it said that bitterness is like drinking poison and waiting for the other person to *die*[19]. Studies have shown that a lifestyle of anger and bitterness has also been attributed to increases in blood pressure and heart problems as well as interfering with the body's immune *system*[20].

We need to bring our anger to the Lord and ask Him to be our justifier, our protector and to fight our battles for us. We are called to extend grace to those who wound and offend us. We are to forgive as God has forgiven us and to be slow to anger *(Romans 12:18-21)*.

We must be sure that the door to our heart is shut tight to the enemy and that when he comes to find an entrance into our lives, all he finds are securely locked doors. We can do this by guarding our heart.

*Read **Proverbs 4:23** and fill in the blanks.*
_____ your _____ with all _____, for out of it spring the _____ of life.

Let's do a little word study here if you don't mind. The Hebrew Lexicon says that the word *keep*[21] can also be translated as to guard or watch over. It can mean to be blockaded (*I especially like that!*). It is the picture of one who stands guard or stands as a watchman. This word can speak of the watchfulness of God and His ability to keep His children *(Isaiah 42:6)*. It also refers to our responsibility to be guarding and keeping our heart from sin and to keep God's ways before us so that we do not stumble.

We are told to guard our heart with all diligence. There is a prayer I pray often, *Lord, help me to be diligent, disciplined and determined.* To diligently guard our heart means that we must work consistently and with effort. We have to pay attention to our words, our thoughts and our actions. We have to be quick to repent and turn from sin. We also must be diligent to study the Word so that it searches our hearts to shine the light upon sin in our life *(Psalm 139:23)*.

Doors can be opened through obvious sins such as adultery, pornography, stealing, lying, etc. But, like Michael in our story, a door can be opened when we are not guarding our heart against fear. God warns us time and again in the Word, "Do not fear!" *(Isaiah 41:10)* Our hearts are to trust securely in Him for all things including protection, provision, circumstances, and even our relationships.

Skandalon

"Mom, don't you think that's a little legalistic? I mean if my sins are paid for, why do I have to worry about opening doors to the enemy? When I pray for forgiveness, doesn't God forgive me and shut those doors?"

"Of course, He forgives you. However, you can be a forgiven child of God and still be walking in bondage to the enemy in areas of your life. Fear, doubt, and unbelief, anger, being unwilling to forgive…any of these can be opportunities for the enemy to get a foothold in your life, even though in other areas you may be walking in obedience. Our words, the Bible says, can bring forth life or death. By speaking negatively, or what the world has to say instead of what the word of God has to say, we can give Satan occasion to bring death into our life. Spiritual as well as physical death."

Michael pondered his mother's words. "The word says God has given us authority over the enemy. Maybe, when we fail to speak and act in faith, we forfeit that authority. I know I've always allowed fear to minister to me. I don't know why I give into it so easily. Even when I try to fight against it, sometimes it's too hard to be constantly guarding my mind and my mouth, and I give up and let fear and worry overtake me." A thought suddenly came to him. "You know, Mom, I was always so afraid of losing Zoe. I knew Amos didn't think I was good enough for her. She was used to living at a higher financial status than I could provide for her, and she's so beautiful. I felt like I lucked out when she agreed to marry me, but I always feared the day she'd realize she'd made a huge mistake in doing so."

Page 139-140

Proverbs 29:25 The fear of man brings a snare, but whoever trusts in the Lord shall be safe.

Speaking of relationships…wrong relationships can open the door to the enemy. I used to tell my children, "*If you hang around a skunk, you're gonna smell like a skunk.*"

God kept Israel separated from the world for a reason. He didn't want them to be contaminated by the world's false gods, corrupt morals, and impure character. Scripture warns us that we are not to be unequally yoked with unbelievers *(2 Corinthians 6:14)*. Our lives can be influenced by those with whom we spend our time. We may work with or have as neighbors those who have not given their lives to Christ. Many of our acquaintances may be unbelievers. However, we must be sure that we are a Godly influence and witness to them and not allow them to draw us into following the ways of the world.

It's important that we keep close to our heart those who will encourage us in our faith walk and help keep us accountable to the Word of God *(Proverbs 22:24-25)*.

Read 1 Corinthians 15:33 and fill in the blanks.
Do not be _____: *"Evil* _____
_____ *good habits."*

Read Proverbs 12:26 and fill in the blanks.
The _____ *should choose his* _____
carefully, for the way of the _____ *leads them astray.*

Even some relationships with those who call themselves Christians can be unhealthy. We must seek God regarding our relationships. If you have friends who are always negative, backbiting or gossiping, judging others, or causing discord in the church they can tempt you to enter into the same sins.

We are to be careful what we allow to enter our eye gate, as well as our ear gate. In *Psalm 101:3, David declared, "I will set nothing wicked before my eyes."*

Television, the internet, video games, and movies are not bad, in and of themselves. However, if we are using these forms of entertainment in such a way that we are corrupted in our beliefs, led astray by the enemy, or forging wrong relationships and thought patterns, they can become keys for the enemy to use to unlock spiritual doors and enter our lives. I have witnessed two marriages that have ended because one of the spouses had an online affair that led to divorce. The affairs were certainly not the fault of a computer. However, the enemy used the computer as a tool to ensnare the intended victims.

We need to examine our lives for generational sins and curses that have been passed down through our lineage. Addictions, wrong life patterns that we see in several of our family members, abandonment or rejection issues by one or both parents, etc. can all result from generational curses. Generational curses or sins are sin patterns that are passed down from one generation to another because they have never been dealt with spiritually. You can close the door to the enemy in your generation so that he cannot affect the lives of your children or the generations that follow (*we'll talk more in detail about this in Week Eight*) .

A lack of knowing the Word and little or no intimacy with the Father is a huge area of entrance to the enemy *(Hosea 4:6)*. When we are intimately acquainted with Christ, seeking His wisdom and direction daily, we have a greater level of discernment and, therefore, are less likely to participate knowingly in sin through open doors.

We can open the door to sickness and disease in our lives by not guarding our words, consistently making wrong food choices or having poor eating habits, choosing not to exercise our body, unforgiveness, and through unconfessed sin *(James 5:16)*. Seeking pity and the attention of others by constantly talking about our ailments will also open the door to infirmity.

Rebellion against God and even the law of the land, ungodly beliefs, and participating in new age religious activities (*Ouija boards, horoscopes, fortune tellers, black magic, etc.*) can all be a means for the enemy to bring destruction in our life.

The bottom line of this lesson is to guard your heart. Though there are many; we've only touched on a few ways that we can open doors and give entrance to the enemy. Therefore, it's important to ask God on a regular basis if you have opened any doors. Be quick to close them by asking for forgiveness, breaking bad habits and renewing your mind by the power of the Holy Spirit. Satan is a legalist, and areas of unconfessed sin give him legal ground in our lives *(1 John 1:9)*.

With absolutely no shame or condemnation, can you think of any doors you have opened to the enemy? Ask God to reveal them to you. Write them down.

_____

_____

_____

_____

_____

_____

_____

Please pray the following prayer in order to slam these doors shut!
Father God, I confess that I have opened the door to the enemy by _____

_____

_____.

I ask for Your forgiveness and repent of this sin. I choose to close the door and ask You to help me renew my mind in this area of my life. I break the power of this sin off of my life. I choose to forgive (name of a person) _____. *(Sometimes you need to forgive yourself or someone else that has offended you, participated in the sin with you, etc.) I break any generational curses associated with this sin and break the power of this sin off of the lives of my descendants. I declare this door to be closed and that the enemy no longer has an entrance into my life in this area. I thank You for the grace to walk out my freedom and victory. You are the God who restores and makes all things new, so I ask You to redeem this area of my life. I now plead the Blood of Jesus over myself and proclaim that I am cleansed by the Blood of the Lamb. Father, I now receive Your forgiveness, love, and freedom from this sin. In Jesus' name, Amen!*

Day 4

For he is cast into a net by his own feet, And he walks into a snare. Job 18:8

Traps and Snares

The very nature of a trap is that it is disguised to look inviting. Traps do not appear to be threatening, but rather they are appealing for the sole purpose of enticing an innocent victim. When we set mouse traps, for example, we put a nice little piece of cheese into the trap because we know that mice love cheese (*or at least we think they do*). The poor little unsuspecting mouse is then drawn into the trap because he can't resist. Satan does the same thing to believers. He desires to take you captive and make you his prisoner.

Please read Matthew 16:21-23. Here in this passage, Jesus is telling His disciples that He is going to have to die for the sins of this world. He's trying to prepare them and yet, also give them hope that He will rise again on the third day. Peter, bless his heart (*that's what we say here in the South*), begins to rebuke Jesus. Look at *Matthew 16:22, "Far be it from You, Lord; this shall not happen to You!"*

Have you ever thought that you could be setting a friend up for a trap of the enemy? Or, possibly, your friend who thinks that they are encouraging you by giving you their advice or opinion, is setting a trap for you. The conversation might go something like this:

"God wants you to be happy…you have every right to be angry and offended. I don't think God wants you to put up with that. If I were you, I'd just leave that church!"

Sometimes we think we are encouraging people when the very situation God has them in may be exactly where He needs them to be to develop His character in their lives.

If Jesus had listened to and been influenced by Peter and decided that He didn't need to go to the cross, where would we be today? If He had decided that He didn't need to suffer and die for humanity and that He didn't need to cover our sins with His blood…where would we be? We would still be lost in our sin!

When we are teaching or trying to encourage others, when we give advice or speak into the lives of others, we must be very careful that we are not speaking the opinions of man. We are wise to speak only as we are led by the Spirit of God.

Jesus loved Peter, yet He likened him to Satan *(Matthew 16:23)*. Peter didn't have God's heart when he spoke to Jesus. He was allowing the enemy to use him in the hopes of trapping Jesus into thinking that He didn't have to go to the cross. Jesus called him an offense. The word *offense*[22] is the Greek word *skandalon*. It means an offense, stumbling block, snare or trap. It speaks of the movable trigger or stick of a trap.

Interestingly enough, this word is often used in reference to Christ. Look at **Romans 9:30-33** and **1 Corinthians 1:18-25**.

Who is the stumbling stone or block to which these Scriptures refer? _____
Why do you think He was considered a stumbling block to the Jews? _____
_____
_____

The religious leaders of Jesus' day were trapped by their opinions as to who the Messiah would be. Because they sought to attain a right relationship with God based on the law instead of by faith, they missed the very One who could save their souls.

Religion can be a huge trap for us. We get caught up in doing what we feel like we need to do to feel *clean* or *good enough*. The religious leaders of Jesus' day were great at doing good works, but there was no genuine love or worship of God motivating their actions. They had a whole list of rules without a truly meaningful relationship.

On the other hand, we can also become trapped into thinking that religion is simply being spiritual. Many good people think that it doesn't matter what we believe in, as long as we believe in *a god*. Satan is constantly trying to muddy the waters of our faith. Through the media, he proposes the lie that there are many roads that lead to God. A dangerous trap that can lead one straight to hell.

*Read **Psalm 91:3** and fill in the blanks.*
Surely He shall deliver you from the _____ *of the* _____
and from the perilous pestilence.

A fowler is one who catches birds in a trap or a snare. The fowler represents Satan. His goal is to set the trap with just the right bait that's going to entice us to waltz right into his snare.

Satan has no limit to the number of traps and snares that he can set for God's people, and he knows exactly what to use to get your eyes off of the Lord and onto the juicy bait he's set before you.

*Read **2 Corinthians 2:11** and fill in the blanks.*
Lest Satan should _____ _____ *of us; for we are not ignorant of*

his _____.

Skandalon

"Convince them that there is more than one way to their God and that to think otherwise is hateful and narrow-minded. Utilize the perceived freedom of other religions to draw and entice them away from the truth of their God. Persuade them that to truly walk in love, they must embrace the beliefs of others, and that to do so pleases Jehovah."

Page 11-12

If we are ignorant of Satan's devices, he can take advantage of us. The words *take advantage of*[3] in this Scripture means to outwit, to trick, or to take advantage of someone through some sinister or sneaky means. Satan may not be able to entrap me with the same methods he uses to entrap you.

A common trap that the enemy uses against us is busyness. I once saw an acronym for the word busy: **B**eing **U**nder **S**atan's **Y**oke. We can be so busy that we have no time for intimacy with God or fellowship with the body of Christ. We can even be busy doing good things but if we are too busy for God…we are simply too busy.

When we become so busy that we can't spend time in the Word or fellowship with the Lord, our spiritual growth can become stunted, and our ability to hear God's voice can become diminished.

Skandalon

"Keep them so preoccupied with their lives that they'll be too distracted to seek after their God. Busyness will lead them to spiritual barrenness. Make sure their jobs, families, children's activities, and their hobbies are so demanding of their time that they have none left at the end of the day for worship of Jehovah. I don't even mind if they follow after godly well-meaning pursuits as long as they stay too busy to pray."

Page 11

Worry is a trap. Jesus told us that we were not to worry *(Matthew 6:25-34)*. If I am not careful, it is very easy for me to be caught in the trap of worry *(my family would shout a hearty, "Amen!")*. As women, we tend to worry about our children and grandchildren. We worry about finances…will there be enough money to pay the bills? How will I buy clothes for my children? Will my children serve the Lord? Will they find the perfect spouse?

Worry is nothing more than a lack of faith in God to meet our needs and to take care of everything that concerns us.

Even as I write this study, I have had to deal with worry in regards to my book, *Skandalon*. The enemy would love nothing more but for me to constantly worry and fret over whether or not this book will be a success. Every day, I have to put it into God's hands and trust Him that if He had me write it, it's His responsibility to ensure that it reaches those He's ordained it to reach.

We can get caught up in seeking the things of this world instead of the things of the Kingdom. Satan desires for you to be driven to seeking after position, status, and power instead of doing the will of God. Our quest of amassing possessions, bigger houses and faster cars can be a trap of the enemy.

> *But seek first the kingdom of God and His righteousness, and all these things shall be added to you.*
> Matthew 6:33

There is a lie that desperately ensnares many women today into thinking that to be beautiful; they must look like the picture of the pencil-thin models in the magazines. It has led to numerous eating disorders, self-hate, and insecurity.

Performance can be a trap the enemy uses to keep you more concerned with being perfect than you are about resting in the love and care of the Father. He'll try to convince you that you should constantly be striving to be better and do better. His lie states that you have to earn God's love and approval. He'll try to convince you to compare yourself with others. He'll make you feel like you are inferior. He'll tell you that God is mad at you, disappointed in you or has given up on you.

All traps keep us from worshipping God with all of our heart, all of our mind and all of our being. They are very craftily designed to distract you from the things of God as well as fulfilling your purpose and destiny.

As I mentioned earlier in this lesson, Satan has many ways in which he can ensnare us. We must stay before the Father, seeking His face and His wisdom to know if we have been caught like a bird in the fowler's net.

The traps the enemy sets for us are often infused with just enough truth from the Word *(trust me, he knows the Word)* that they appear to be acceptable and desirable. He is famous for this tactic.

Once you become trapped, it's often very difficult to find freedom. Obviously, the key is to avoid his traps. The best way to stay free is to know his strategies.

*Read **Ephesians 6:11** and fill in the blanks.*
Put on the _____ _____ of God, that you may be able to _____ against the _____ of the devil.

We must daily put on the whole armor of God and stand against the wiles of Satan.

The word *wiles*[24] according to Merriam-Webster's online dictionary is defined as a trick or stratagem intended to ensnare or deceive.

It is necessary that we daily examine our hearts and ask God to reveal anything that is a weight, sin or trap that would keep us from fulfilling our destiny. We need to pray to walk in the wisdom of God.

*Read **Hebrews 12:1-2** and fill in the blanks.*
Therefore we also, since we are surrounded by so great a cloud of witnesses, let us lay aside every _____, and the _____ which so easily _____ us, and let us _____ _____ _____ the race that is set before us, looking unto _____, the author and finisher of our faith, who for the joy that was set before Him endured the cross, despising the shame, and has sat down at the right hand of the throne of God.

A weight is anything that entangles us and keeps us from doing God's will.

The word *ensnare*[25] in this passage is a word that means to be skillfully surrounded, to prevent or retard running. It carries the idea of something that comfortably stands all around you, such as a comfortable environment. Satan's traps often feel so comfortable and familiar that we don't recognize that we are caught in his snare.

The key I want you to get from this Scripture is that we are to keep our eyes on Christ. Keeping our focus on Christ and His Word will certainly make it more difficult for the enemy to ensare us.

Can you think of any ways in which the enemy has you snared in a trap?
If so, write them down. If not, pray and ask God to reveal to you if you might be trapped and yet don't even perceive it. Write down what He shows you.

Day 5

For if you live according to the flesh you will die; but if by the Spirit you put to death the deeds of the body, you will live. Romans 8:13

MY FLESH CRIES OUT!

Desperate situations, tumultuous storms and deep pits may be the result of us catering to our flesh. We often blame the devil for the bad things happening in our lives that have occurred as a result of our stubborn flesh wanting to have its way. Satan certainly may be the blame for the temptation that presents itself to us, but we are at fault for yielding to that temptation. For instance, I might be tempted to have an extramarital affair, but I have a choice to make as to how I will respond to that temptation. We all are faced with situations that are tempting, but that doesn't mean we have to succumb to the temptation.

We know that the Holy Spirit led Jesus into the wilderness to be tempted immediately following His baptism by John. He did not yield to the temptation but used God's Words to oppose the enemy.

*Please read **Hebrews 4:14-15** and fill in the blanks.*
Seeing then that we have a great High Priest who has passed through the heavens, Jesus the Son of God, let us _____ _____ our confession. For we do not have a High Priest who cannot _____ with our _____, but was in _____ points _____ as we are, yet _____ sin.

Jesus faced temptation just as each one of us must face temptations. Yet, He was without sin. If you are a child of God, you have His nature living in you and, by the power of the Holy Spirit, the ability to resist temptation just as He did.

Read James 1:12-15. Let's make one thing clear; God is not the tempter of the brethren. Satan is the tempter *(Matthew 4:3)*. Any enticement to do evil comes from the enemy of our souls. However, we have the ability to overcome every temptation. We sin when we submit to and act upon unholy and ungodly desires.

*Please fill in the blank by looking at **James 1:14-15**.*
But each one is tempted when he is _____ _____ by his own

_____ _and_ _____. _Then, when desire has_ _____, _it gives birth to_ _____; _and sin, when it is full-grown, brings forth_ _____.

The temptation in and of itself is not sinful. As a matter of fact, you can't grow in your faith walk if you are never tempted or tested. When reading the Word, you will find that every giant of the faith faced times of testing and temptation. It is how spiritual muscles develop, and spiritual growth takes place in the life of the believer. It's when we give in to the desires of our flesh that we step into sin. Unless we are quick to repent and turn from that sin, it will bring forth spiritual death.

The phrase _is drawn away_[26] carries the meaning of one who is being lured from his or her hiding place. We must stay hidden in the secret place of the Most High, trusting Him to meet our needs daily, allowing Him

> _For you died, and your life is hidden_
> _with Christ in God._
> Colossians 3:3

to lead and guide us, and work out His will in our lives. When we do this, we are promised deliverance from the snare of the fowler. Christ overcame temptation by setting His mind to do the will of His Father.

Look at **Colossians 3:1-2** _and fill in the blanks._
If then you were raised with Christ, _____ _those things which are_ _____, _where Christ is, sitting at the right hand of God._ _____ _____ _____ _on things_ _____, _not on_ _____ _____ _____ _____.

We are most vulnerable to temptation or giving in to our fleshly desires when our minds are focused on our earthly needs and desires.

Read Matthew 26:36-46. In this passage of Scripture, we see Jesus at Gethsemane with His disciples. He knows that His time on earth is coming to an end and what is ahead of Him; He will suffer at the hands of man, carrying the sins of the world and taking them to the cross. He asks His disciples to pray with Him, yet they are tired. It's late, it's dark, and they are having a difficult time staying awake _(been there, done that so I can't judge them)._

Just a word to the wise, we are most weak and vulnerable when we are tired. We need to be sure that we give our bodies the rest they need. We also need to be certain that we are active in the things God calls us to and that we do not get caught up in works to please man.

Jesus gave His disciples a means of avoiding temptation.

85

Read verse 41 and fill in the blanks.
"_____ and _____, *lest you enter into*
_____. *The spirit indeed is willing, but the* _____
is weak."

According to the Greek Lexicon, the word *watch*[27] means that we need to pay strict attention; be cautious and be active. So we must watch for those subtle temptations that the enemy puts before us. But we are also warned to pray lest we enter into temptation.

Spending time in the presence of the Lord strengthens our spirit man making us less vulnerable to the appetites of our flesh. Our flesh wants its way! Given the opportunity to be tempted, if we are not strong in the Lord through our continual communion with Him, our flesh can easily be led astray.

My husband and I have a saying that we often use in our home when we see the other being tempted to be impatient, easily angered, etc. Upon seeing the negative character in one another, one of us will ask the other, "*Have you spent any time in prayer?*" We say it in a light-hearted spirit, but it's a reminder to guard against fleshly behavior.

*Read **Galatians 5:19-21**. Please list the works of the flesh listed in this passage of Scripture.*
_____
_____
_____

_____

Satan cannot force you to sin. However, God will not force you to choose either. He has given you a free will. You make the choice to participate in these fleshly works.

> *I call heaven and earth as witnesses today against you, that I have set before you life and death, blessing and cursing; therefore choose life, that both you and your descendants may live.*
> Deuteronomy 30:19

*Now, please turn to **Galatians 5:24** and fill in the blanks.*
And those who are _____
have _____ *the*
_____ *with its*
passions and _____.

Besides watching and praying as a means to escape temptation, we must crucify the desires of our flesh. How do we do that? We die to them! We trust that God will give us those things that we need and even the desires of our heart. He knows our needs. He knows our thoughts and deepest desires. We have to trust in His loving-kindness and willingness to meet every need.

We can become easily tempted when we believe the lie that God is not good and that He doesn't care about us, our needs, or our desires. We tend to take matters into our own hands, placing ourselves outside of the shelter of the Most High.

Be assured that you have the ability in you to overcome fleshly desires because Christ dwells within you.

In Gethsemane, Christ, when faced with the reality of what was ahead, prayed fervently. He also solicited others to pray with Him. When we are in a season of temptation, we need to do the same. We should not only fervently pray for ourselves, but seek out a trusted member of the body of Christ to pray for and with us.

> But if the Spirit of Him who raised Jesus from the dead dwells in you, He who raised Christ from the dead will also give life to your mortal bodies through His Spirit who dwells in you.
>
> Romans 8:11

Skandalon

Ramiah looked on as Zoe sat on the couch, completely unaware of the demonic presence surrounding her. The enemy's attack was escalating as strongholds were fortified against his charge's life. A proverbial Pandora's box was opened. Anger, Anxiety, Lust, and a host of demons hung around waiting for opportunities to pounce on their unsuspecting prey.

He wanted desperately to slice these scoundrels to pieces, sending them trembling and shrieking in fear as he threw them into the pit. However, he was still held back by her lack of prayer and refusal to call on the Father for deliverance. His beloved charge was ignorant of the enemy's devices. She couldn't feel the invisible chains of bitterness and unforgiveness wrapped around her soul, nor could she see the incredibly intricate web of deceit he was spinning around her. She'd swallowed his lies hook, line, and sinker. Her feet were no longer equipped with the Gospel of peace but bound by shackles of rebellion. Her eyes were blinded to God's infinite love, and her ears could no longer distinguish her Shepherd's voice apart from other voices that clamored for her attention. Worst of all, she couldn't see that His arms were wide open, ready to receive her the moment she turned her life back over to Him.

Page 134

We must continually submit our lives to the power and control of the Holy Spirit so that we can subdue our fleshly desires. If we focus our attention on growing in Christ, He will assist us in daily dying to our self.

*Can you think of any temptations you have overcome in your life? What strategy did you use to overcome the temptations?*_____

_____

_____

_____

_____

_____

What spiritual growth have you seen in your life as a result of overcoming these temptations?

_____

_____

_____

_____

4

Week Four Bible Study

Skandalon Reading assignment: Chapters 13-16

Day 1

For the weapons of our warfare are not carnal but mighty in God for pulling down strongholds.
2 Corinthians 10:4

THE WEAPONS OF OUR WARFARE

As I've said before, it is important for us to remember that Satan is a defeated enemy *(Colossians 2:13-15, Hebrews 2:14-15)*. Christ defeated him by laying down His life on the cross and dying for the sins of all who would, in faith, believe in Him.

Though we will face attacks from the enemy, as we have studied in a previous lesson, we have been given an arsenal of weapons to fight against his schemes.

God has not left us without specific instructions as to how we are to stand against our enemy. Since the battles we face are spiritual battles, it's important that we use spiritual weapons instead of trying to win in our own strength using fleshly weapons.

The Bible states in *Hosea 4:6*, that we are destroyed for a lack of knowledge. A lack of knowledge, as we discussed in *Week Three*, is an open door for the enemy to waltz into our lives and wreak havoc and destruction. We must know his schemes and how to fight against him effectively.

Read Ephesians 6:10-18 and fill in the blanks.

_____, *my brethren, be strong in the Lord and in the* _____
of His might. Put on the _____ *armor of God, that you may be able to*

_____ against the _____ of the devil. For we do not wrestle against _____ _____ _____, but against principalities, against powers, against the rulers of the darkness of this age, against spiritual hosts of wickedness in the _____ _____. Therefore take up the whole armor of God, that you may be able to _____ in the evil day, and having done all, to _____.

_____ therefore, having girded your waist with _____, having put on the breastplate of _____, and having shod your feet with the preparation of the gospel of _____; above all, taking the shield of _____ with which you will be able to quench all the fiery darts of the wicked one. And take the helmet of _____, and the sword of the Spirit, which is the _____ of God; praying always with all prayer and supplication in the Spirit, being watchful to this end with all perseverance and supplication for all the saints—

> I, therefore, the prisoner of the Lord, beseech you to walk worthy of the calling with which you were called, with all lowliness and gentleness, with longsuffering, bearing with one another in love, endeavoring to keep the unity of the Spirit in the bond of peace. There is one body and one Spirit, just as you were called in one hope of your calling;
> Ephesians 4:1-4

Notice that Paul starts out these verses with the word *finally* which indicates that extreme importance is being placed on the statement that follows.

It would seem that the Ephesian church, which was the largest church in its time, was undergoing a spiritual attack. Believers apparently weren't acting very Christ-like *(Can you imagine that?)*. In *Ephesians 4:1-4*, Paul had just finished exhorting the body of believers in Ephesus to walk worthy of their calling, bear with each other in love, and keep the unity of the Spirit. He then taught them about the spiritual armor as a means of standing against the enemy while walking out their Christian faith. This week we will examine the armor one piece at a time.

Being imprisoned and surrounded by soldiers daily, Paul was able to see the effectiveness of each piece of the soldier's armor. He draws a parallel using the uniform of the first-century Roman soldier, to describe the spiritual armor of a Christian.

I generally pray the armor over myself on a daily basis. It helps to remind me that I have everything I need to stand against enemy onslaught. Notice in *Ephesians 6:11*, Paul's instructions warned the church body to put on the whole armor of God. Each piece is significant. Nothing should be forgotten so that the soldier remains well protected.

The word *wiles*[28] in *verse 11* is the Greek word *methodos*. It means *with a road*. The devil has a method of attack against the believer. He's mapped out a plan of attack against you, against the church, against your family…you get the picture! He wants to take you down the wrong road, cause you to detour on your journey and keep you from fulfilling your destiny.

In Ephesians 6:11 and in Ephesians 6:13 we see something repeated. Can you find the similar phrases? _____

_____

_____

Whenever the Holy Spirit repeats something in Scripture, He is putting emphasis on its importance. There is a word that is repeated in *verse 11, verse 13,* and again in *verse 14.*

What is that common word in all three Scriptures? _____

_____

We are called to stand against the enemy. We are not to cower in fear or run in defeat from his attacks. We are to stand in our armor and fight. God has equipped us with all that we need in order to stand until we see our enemy defeated.

The first piece of armor the soldier would put on is the loin belt. Made of tough leather strips and small brass plates for extra protection, it was an adornment as well as a piece of armor. Worn about the loins (*the upper and lower abdominal area and the area of the hips*), this piece of armor shielded some of the most vulnerable parts of the body. The belt held much of the other pieces of armor in place, including the sword.

The belt is used as a metaphor for truth. *Read John 8:31-32 and fill in the blanks.*

Then Jesus said to those Jews who believed Him, "If you _____ in _____ _____, you are My disciples indeed. And you shall know the _____, and the _____ shall make you free."

As Christians, we base our beliefs on the truth of God's Word. Our faith is to be firmly founded on it. Like the belt, God's truth holds everything else together for us. It is our firm foundation.

Satan is the father of all lies and will always attempt to cast doubt on the truth that we know.

Read John 14:6 and fill in the blanks.

Jesus said to him, "I am the way, the _____*, and the life. No one comes to the Father except through Me.*

We live in a world under the influence of the enemy where the validity of God's Word is challenged every day. It is important that you know the truth of God's Word so that you can give an answer to anyone who asks you about the reason for the hope you have in Christ *(1 Peter 3:15)*.

Jesus stated that the Word is the truth *(John 17:17)*. You cannot effectively counter-attack the lies of the enemy unless you know the truth of God's Word. If Satan can get you to doubt the validity of God's Word in any one area, he'll be able to cast doubt in other areas as well.

One lie of the enemy that I believed for years is that God's love for me was conditional. The enemy would torment me when I sinned or felt like I'd disappointed God. He deceived me into believing that God was angry and that I needed to earn back His love.

Another lie that I believed for many years was that my life had no value. I struggled with the idea of suicide because I truly believed that my life was worthless, and I wasn't contributing anything to anyone. I swallowed the lie that my children didn't need me and my husband would be better off without me. I'm thankful that God has exposed the enemy's lies, and I now believe the truth. I am loved by my Father. I am valuable!

*Can you think of any areas in your life where the enemy has tried to cast doubt on the truth of God's Word?*_____

_____

_____

_____

_____

_____

_____

_____

_____

_____

*Read **1 Peter 1:13** and fill in the blanks.*

Therefore _____ _____ _____ _____ *of your*

_____, *be sober, and rest your hope fully upon the grace that is to be brought to you at the revelation of Jesus Christ;*

Skandalon

Michael was spending more time in prayer, drawing closer to the Almighty for strength as he walked through this season of trial. Each new assault made him determined to seek after the Almighty that much more. Though he couldn't perceive it, his relationship with the Almighty was growing by leaps and bounds. He was developing unshakable faith and his spiritual muscles were growing stronger. The Almighty was taking him to new levels of glory though Michael often saw himself as weak and failing in his faith. Deuel knew that the Almighty was pleased with his charge as he hung onto the word in faith and trusted in his heavenly Father's love.

Page 157

To be girded or have the waist girded gives the idea of being in a constant state of readiness or preparation. Our minds must be in a state of ready alert to thwart off the enemy's lies. We must have the Word hidden in our heart so that the Holy Spirit can bring it to our remembrance when needed to stand against an attack.

We are called to walk in the truth of God's Word, know the truth, and speak the truth in love.

> *...but, speaking the truth in love, may grow up in all things into Him who is the head—Christ—*
> *Ephesians 4:15*

I learned very early on in my walk with the Lord that beating someone over the head with the Bible will most likely never win them to Christ. However, when we speak the truth and let our lives be an outward expression of the inward truth that abides within us, demonstrating by our actions His love before the world, they will hunger to know Jesus.

Let's close this lesson out by looking at one last Scripture.

Read 2 Timothy 3:16 and fill in the blanks.
All _____ is given by _____ of God, and is profitable for _____, for _____, for _____, for _____ in righteousness...

Though written by the hands of men, the Bible is God-breathed. Every word on every page has a purpose. It will speak to you, challenge you, comfort, correct, and guide you if you heed the truth spoken within its pages. It promises not to return void *(Isaiah 55:11)*. You can base your eternal destiny on it!

Let's close out with a prayer.

Father,

Today I choose to take up the whole armor of God so that I can stand against the strategies of the enemy. I put on the belt of truth. Your Word is truth. My mind is filled with the truth of Your Word. Your truth is my defense against the enemy. I love Your truth and desire to live by Your truth. Help me to be bold to speak Your truth in love. Let it bring freedom to any wounds in my soul as well as freedom to those to whom I proclaim it. Hypocrisy and lies are far from me. Help me to discern when I am believing the lies of the enemy and not walking in Your truth. In Jesus name, Amen!

Day 2

For they being ignorant of God's righteousness, and seeking to establish their own righteousness, have not submitted to the righteousness of God. Romans 10:3

THE BREASTPLATE OF RIGHTEOUSNESS

*Please review **Ephesians 6:10–18** once again.*

The breastplate, which was sometimes called chainmail, was a crucial piece of the Roman soldier's weaponry. It protected the central organs of the body, particularly the heart and lungs, against attack. It was crafted of solid metal or metal bands and was worn around the chest area like a vest making it difficult for arrows to penetrate through to fatally wound the soldier.

One of Satan's greatest strategies is to convince the believer that he or she is unworthy to be called a child of God. I remember as a young Christian going to the altar to be *saved* over and over again, hoping that at some point it would *take*. Because I was not rooted and grounded in the Word, Satan had convinced me that I was unclean, unworthy and that I needed to work my way into God's graces. Even as I matured in my walk with God, it took years to be free from this lie. For much longer than I'd like to confess, I never felt *good enough* and lived under constant condemnation.

We are instructed in *Proverbs 4:23* to guard our heart. Therefore, we must daily put on the breastplate of righteousness. If the enemy can convince you that you are not righteous, he can keep you from victory in so many other areas of your life.

Skandalon

"Amos, God takes us just as we are. You don't ever have to worry about changing for God to accept you. He loves you just as you are. He's changed me because the more I've fallen in love with Him, the more I want to change for Him so that I'm pleasing to Him."

Pages 169-170

Read 2 Corinthians 5:21 and fill in the blanks.
For He made Him who knew no sin to be sin for us, that we might become the _____
_____ *of God in* _____.

Through His surrender to the Father and death on the cross, Jesus became your righteousness. If you have accepted His sacrifice, you are made righteous in Him.

According to the Greek Lexicon, the word *righteousness*[29] means that you are made acceptable to God. You are in right standing with Him. You didn't do anything to earn this state of righteousness, and you can't possibly do anything to keep yourself in it. So faith in the righteousness that Christ has appropriated for us is a powerful spiritual weapon.

A subtle lie of the enemy is that you must earn your righteousness. He would have you believe that there are rules you must follow, dress codes to be adhered to, church attendance records that must be kept, and good deeds that are being tallied in heaven. All in an effort to earn your good-standing with the Father.

Read Romans 3:20-24 and fill in the blanks.
Therefore by the _____ *of the law no* _____ *will be*
_____ *in His sight, for by the law is the knowledge of sin.*
But now the _____ *of God apart from the law is revealed, being witnessed*
by the Law and the Prophets, even the righteousness of God, through _____ *in Jesus*
Christ, to all and on all who _____. *For there is no difference; for* _____ *have*
sinned and _____ _____ *of the glory of God, being justified* _____
by His _____ *through the redemption that is in Christ Jesus,*

The word *justified*[30] means to be declared righteous! Just as if you had never sinned. When we place our trust in the faithfulness of God to save us, we must believe by faith that we are completely justified. We are made righteous because of the redeeming work of Christ. If we don't fully understand this truth, Satan will place us in a prison where freedom is earned through hard labor.

Does that mean we are free to sin without consequence? No! When we sin, as we discussed in our earlier lessons, we open the door to the enemy and will suffer the consequences of our sins. However, God will do everything within His power (*and He has much more power than our enemy…it's not even a contest!*) to draw us back to Himself and on the road to fulfilling our destiny.

Our spiritual father, Abraham, is a good example of this principle. When God spoke a promise to Abram *(Genesis 12:1-3, Genesis 15:1-7)*, he simply took God at His Word.

*Read **Romans 4:1-3** and then read **Romans 4:20-22** and fill in the blanks.*
What then shall we say that Abraham our father has found according to the flesh? For if Abraham was justified by _____, he has something to boast about, but not before God. For what does the Scripture say? "Abraham believed God, and it was accounted to him for _____."
He did not _____ at the promise of God through unbelief, but was strengthened in faith, giving glory to God, and being _____ _____ that what He had promised He was also able to perform. And therefore "it was accounted to him for _____."

Abraham believed in the promises of God. He didn't doubt that God would keep the covenant He'd made with him. Therefore, he was made righteous or in right standing with God.

*Now read **Romans 4:23-25** and fill in the blanks.*
Now it was not written for his sake alone that it was _____ to him, but also for _____. It shall be _____ to _____ who _____ in Him who raised up Jesus our Lord from the dead, who was delivered up because of our _____, and was raised because of our justification.

The word *imputed*[31] simply means credited. We are credited with being righteous in the sight of God when we place our faith in Jesus Christ as our Savior. Look at **Romans 5:1**: *Having been justified by faith, we have peace with God through our Lord Jesus Christ.*

The enemy hates this truth and the believer who walks in the knowledge of it. He'll do all he can to keep your focus on earning God's love instead of walking in the blessings that are yours. God has purchased your freedom, but Satan wants you to believe the lie that you must strive to earn it.

*Read **Philippians 3:8-9** and fill in the blanks.*
Yet indeed I also count all things loss for the excellence of the knowledge of Christ Jesus my Lord, for whom I have suffered the loss of all things, and count them as rubbish, that I may gain Christ and be found in Him, not having my own _____, which is from the _____, but that which is through _____ in Christ, the righteousness which is from _____ by _____.

The breastplate of righteousness also guards our heart against sin. Even though we are in

> *Let us therefore come boldly to the throne of grace, that we may obtain mercy and find grace to help in time of need.*
> *Hebrews 4:16*

right standing with God, we all occasionally sin. When we find that we have sinned before God, we can come boldly to the throne of grace and obtain mercy and forgiveness.

Repentance is important in keeping our heart protected. Make no mistake about it; God is never indifferent to our sin. He requires obedience. However, obedience is always for our protection and is a means of keeping the enemy from gaining entrance to our heart.

*Look at **James 1:21-25** and fill in the blanks.*

Therefore lay aside all _____ and overflow of _____, and receive with meekness the _____ _____, which is able to save your souls. But be _____of the _____, and not _____ only, _____ yourselves. For if anyone is a _____ of the word and not a _____, he is like a man observing his natural face in a mirror; for he observes himself, goes away, and immediately forgets what kind of man he was. But he who looks into the perfect _____ _____ _____ and _____ in it, and is not a forgetful hearer but a _____ of the work, this one will be _____ in what he does.

We are to be (*obedient*) doers of the Word because we are blessed when we are obedient. We are called to be like Christ. That transformation takes place as we allow the Word of God to take root in our heart and change us from glory to glory. We are not called to be doers of the Word out of fear of failure or displeasing God. Rather, we should be motivated to be doers out of a grateful heart, filled with a love for our Father and Savior.

God promises that He will never leave us or forsake us. However, we can walk out from under the umbrella of His protection and, therefore, become vulnerable to the enemy and his ability to ensnare us.

When we are walking in obedience to the Word, our heart does not condemn us, and we can receive freely from God.

*Read **1 John 3:18-23** and fill in the blanks.*

My little children, let us not love in word or in tongue, but in _____ and in truth. And by this we know that we are of the _____, and shall assure our hearts before Him.

For if our heart condemns us, God is greater than our heart, and knows all things. Beloved, if our heart does not condemn us, we have _____ toward God. And whatever we ask we _____ from Him, because we _____ His commandments and _____ those things that are _____ in His sight. And this is His commandment: that we should believe on the name of His Son Jesus Christ and love one another, as He gave us commandment.

Let's close out the day with this prayer:

Father, I thank you that I am the righteousness of God in Christ Jesus. I put on the breastplate of righteousness and stand in the righteousness of Christ. Therefore, I can come boldly before the throne of grace to receive every good and perfect gift from You. There is now no condemnation for me because I walk and live in the truth of Your Word. No weapon formed against me can prosper and every tongue that rises against me in judgment I shall condemn. My righteousness is from the Lord. I rest in You today.

Day 3

For He Himself is our peace, who has made both one, and has broken down the middle wall of separation... Ephesians 2:14

SANDALS OF PEACE

*Please read **Ephesians 6:15** and fill in the blanks.*
And having _____ your _____ with the preparation of the _____ of _____ ;

A very important piece of armor for the Roman soldier was his shoes or sandals. Now, most of my sweet sisters will understand the language of shoes. You don't wear tennis shoes to a formal party, and you certainly wouldn't wear a cute pair of red heels to walk the hiking trails in the National Forest. There are as many different types of shoes as there are occasions and outfits to wear them (*can I get a great big hallelujah!!!*).

For our spiritual armor to be complete, we must have on our sandals of peace. Having once visited Israel, I know that much of the terrain is rough and rocky. It would be difficult for a soldier to maneuver without the proper sandals. These leather sandals laced up the center of the foot and up onto the ankle. The thick soles of the sandals were equipped with spikes. In the midst of the battle, the soldier would drive the spikes into the rocky ground enabling him to stand in his place as he fought against the enemy.

Satan's goal is to wear the body of Christ down so that we will run in retreat. He will often attack the believer with multiple attacks, one right after the other. However, we must not grow battle weary. We are called to stand until the battle is won.

We are told to shod (*put on*) our feet the preparation of the Gospel of peace. The Holy Spirit calls each of us to a place of preparation in Christ. We become prepared by being intimate with the One Who promises peace, knowing the Gospel of peace, and allowing it to take root in our spirit and soul.

It is interesting that God would tell us to equip ourselves with peace. I believe that the Holy Spirit used the metaphor of the sandal to remind us that we can be at peace in any situation we are walking in or through because Satan is under our feet.

*Read **Romans 16:20** and fill in the blanks.*
And the God of _____ will crush Satan _____ _____

_____ *shortly. The grace of our Lord Jesus Christ be with you. Amen.*

Satan desires to steal your peace. He knows that you can't walk in faith and love if you are fearful, agitated, distressed, and angry. You will not be an overcomer and, therefore, a witness to anyone if you are constantly walking in unrest or allowing vain imaginations to control your thought life.

Let's look at one definition of the Greek word *eirene,* which translates as *peace.*[32] The tranquil state of a soul assured of its salvation through Christ, and so fearing nothing from God and content with its earthly lot, of whatsoever sort that is. To be at peace is to be at rest, in a state of quietness and calm even in the midst of difficult circumstances. The definition also includes being at peace with God and man. We can walk in peace because we are children of the Prince of Peace.

Though we are told that we will walk through trials on this earth, we are assured that God will walk with us through them and grace us to overcome them. Peace comes as we trust in Him and His ability to meet every need, fix what has been broken, heal every hurt, and go to battle on our behalf. When we trust, He will give us peace in the midst of the darkest storms.

We are exhorted to let His peace rule in our hearts.

*Read **Colossians 3:15** and fill in the blanks.*
And let the _____ of God rule in your hearts, to which also you were called in one body; and be thankful.

The word *rule*[33] in this Scripture refers to an umpire. It can also be translated as to decide, determine or control. God's peace is to be the deciding factor in every situation of life. If I don't have peace about a situation I'm seeking the Lord on, I will not move forward until I have it. Christ promises to give peace to us.

How do we let the peace of God rule in our hearts, you might ask? By abiding in Him and casting our cares upon Him. We are also to trust Him implicitly in every situation. I have come to walk in more and more peace as I've grown in my relationship with Him. Having witnessed Him move mightily on my behalf on so many different occasions, I know that He is faithful to care for me. I don't always see Him moving in my situation right away, but I know that as soon as I pray…He steps into the midst of the storm and sends a calming peace.

The greatest example of this in my life is when my husband received a diagnose of stage four colon cancer. Immediately upon hearing the news of such a devastating diagnosis, fear tried to penetrate my heart. But as soon as my husband and I came home from receiving the doctor's report, I pulled out my Bible and opened directly to a passage of Scripture that promised long life for my man. The peace of God enveloped me from that moment on, and I knew that I knew Joe would be fine. We went through chemo, radiation, and surgery, but at the time of this writing, over ten years later…he is still cancer free.

*Read **Philippians 4:6-7** and fill in the blanks.*

Be _____ for _____, but in _____ by _____ and supplication, with thanksgiving, let your requests be made known to God; and the _____ of God, which _____ all _____, will guard your hearts and minds through Christ Jesus.

Skandalon

"I will walk by faith and not by sight! I don't care what she says or what she does…nothing is too difficult for God! I will trust You, Lord. In faith, I worship You, Almighty God. I worship You. I choose to trust You."

Peace, like a warm blanket of love wrapped around his wounded soul, enveloped him,

melting away the anger.

"You are my peace that surpasses my understanding."

Page 166

God's peace will guard our heart and mind when we surrender all fear and anxiety over to Him. However, be assured the enemy will fight you tooth and nail to keep you from walking in peace. We will talk about the thought life in another lesson, but you must guard your thoughts. Keep your focus on Christ and the finished work of the cross.

*Read **Romans 10:14-15** and fill in the blanks.*

How then shall they call on Him in whom they have not _____? And how shall they believe in Him of whom they have not _____? And how shall they hear without a _____? And how shall they preach unless they are sent? As it is written:"How beautiful are the feet of those who preach the gospel of _____, who bring glad tidings of good things!"

We live in the midst of a chaotic world where there are religions that justify the killing of anyone who does not agree with their beliefs; it is good to know that we serve a God of peace.

Our Gospel is the Gospel of peace. We may not agree with the lifestyles or decisions of others, but we are called to be peacemakers (*Romans 12:18*). Therefore, we are always to share the Gospel in love. We are not called to hate those who disagree with us but to show them the love of Christ by our words and actions. We are to trust in the Holy Spirit to do the life-changing work on their souls as we reach out in love. It is not our job to save anyone.

> *Blessed are the peacemakers, For they shall be called sons of God.*
> *Matthew 5:9*

We are to present the Gospel and be a living example of God's love and peace. The Holy Spirit will do the rest.

If we are presenting ourselves as hateful, prejudiced, antagonistic, or disrespectful of others, it is highly unlikely that the lost will want to follow after our God. We are called to be His hands and feet to this generation; Jesus with skin on. Our words are to be compassionate and love-filled. We are to be a light that shines in the midst of a dark world.

One of the names of God is Jehovah Shalom. He is the God Who promises peace to His children. True peace only comes through a relationship with Him.

Today, rest in His peace. Please say this prayer out loud:

Jehovah Shalom, God of peace, I thank You that I can rest in You today. I surrender every trial and difficult situation over to You trusting that You are well able to meet every need. I know that You have promised to walk with me through the valleys and give me peace in the midst of storms. I put the sandals of peace on my spiritual feet today. I choose to walk in peace and will not allow agitation or fear a place in my thought life. I will walk in peace with those who cross my path today, being a demonstration of Your mercy and love. Strife and offense have no place in my heart. Your peace will rule and reign in my heart today. Thank You that I have victory in every situation. In Jesus name, Amen!

Day 4

For by grace you have been saved through faith, and that not of yourselves; it is the gift of God,
Ephesians 2:8

SHIELD OF FAITH

The battle shield of a Roman soldier was large and rectangular though curved on the edges. It was sturdy and made from three pieces of wood glued together and covered with leather. It is believed that the soldier would drench the leather before battle so that the flaming arrows of the enemy would be quenched as they made contact with the shield. The fact that the shield was wide and long gave it the ability to cover the Roman soldier completely.

*Review **Ephesians 6:16** and fill in the blanks.*
Above all, taking the shield of _____ with which you will be able to quench all the _____ _____ of the wicked one.

Faith is essential to the life of the believer. Without faith, it is impossible to please God. Faith believes God above all other voices and the negative circumstances that confront us. Our faith must be centered in Christ and His atoning work on the cross. As we discussed last week, one of the greatest strategies of the enemy is to get you to doubt your salvation, your right-standing in Christ, and your identity as a son or daughter of God. It is essential that we know what God's Word says about our standing in Christ.

Think back to the day of your salvation experience. Please briefly write down how you came to know Christ as your Lord and Savior. If you know the date, please write that down as well.

_____

_____

_____

_____

_____

_____

Now, when the enemy tries to convince you that you are not saved (*and he will*), refer to the above entry and then tell him to get lost!

We all face doubts from time to time. We wonder if God sees our situation and hears our cries for help, if He has enough resources to meet our needs, or if He desires to do the impossible for us. I don't know about you, but I've always had faith to believe God to meet the needs of others, yet I often struggle to muster enough faith to see my needs met. The reason for this is because I know my heart! The enemy would love for us to believe that we are not good enough to see the goodness of God in our life. He would have us believe the lie that God cares for others while He chooses to ignore our needs. He's a liar!

Read Ephesians 3:16-19 and fill in the blanks.
That He would grant you, according to the riches of His glory, to be strengthened with might through His Spirit in the inner man, that Christ may dwell in your hearts through _____; that you, being rooted and grounded in _____, may be able to comprehend with all the saints what is the width and length and depth and height— to know the _____ of Christ which passes knowledge; that you may be _____ with all the _____ of God.

I believe that the Apostle Paul prayed this prayer over the Church of the Ephesians because they, like us, struggled to know the love of God. We can't possibly walk in faith if we don't understand the love that the Father has for us. Our shield is rendered ineffective. He loves us so much that He sent His One and only Son to die an excruciatingly painful death on our behalf.

Skandalon

He sat on the edge of his bed, thumbing through Zoe's Bible. He'd found it while cleaning out her nightstand. It grieved him that she'd left it behind. Michael opened the Bible to the page marked by an embroidered bookmark; a gift from Grandma Abby. A scripture caught his attention. Apparently, the highlighted scripture had been special to Zoe. He read it out loud several times.
"For I am persuaded that neither death nor life, nor angels nor principalities nor powers, nor things present nor things to come, nor height nor depth, nor any other created thing, shall be able to separate us from the love of God which is in Christ Jesus our Lord."
Page 178

*Read **Galatians 5:6** and fill in the blanks.*
For in Christ Jesus neither circumcision nor uncircumcision avails anything, but
_____ *working through* _____.

I have heard many say that this Scripture teaches us that if we are not walking in love, our faith is hindered. I believe this to be true. However, I also believe that this passage teaches us that if we doubt the love of God for ourselves, our faith will be disrupted. We must be grounded in the reality of God's unconditional love for us to walk by faith in the promises of God. If you don't believe that God is good, how can you possibly believe He will do good things for you?

By faith, we are to stand in the belief that God loves us unconditionally and unequivocally (*we will devote an entire lesson to this truth in Week Seven*). Nothing can separate the believer from His love. His love for you is everlasting, meaning it will never fail *(2 Thessalonians 2:16)*. He has promised that He will never leave you or forsake you.

*Read **Romans 10:17** and fill in the blanks.*
So then _____ *comes by* _____, *and hearing by the*
_____ _____ _____.

If you are a born-again child of God, you had someone present the Gospel message to you, either personally, you heard it preached, or you read it from the Bible. Your faith for salvation was awakened when you heard the Word of God.

Faith to believe God for our daily needs, healing, deliverance, the salvation of a loved one, the restoration of your marriage, etc. comes from hearing the Word of God. For this reason, I often pray the Word out loud. Sometimes, I even read the Bible out loud. It is a faith builder. The Word is the foundation of our faith. The more we hear and read it, the stronger our faith becomes.

I have often likened faith to a checking account. When you read and study the Word or listen to the preaching of the Word, it is like putting money into a checking account. Therefore, when a need arises, you will have something from which to withdraw. However, if you find yourself in a desperate situation where faith is needed, but you haven't been faithful to put the Word into your spiritual account, your account will be empty. You'll find it very difficult to walk in faith.

*Read **2 Corinthians 5:7** and fill in the blanks.*

For we walk by _____, not by _____.

Satan desires to keep you focused on your natural circumstances and, therefore, become hopeless. However, faith doesn't look at what it sees in the natural. Faith enables us to keep our eyes focused on God and His power. Nothing is too difficult for Him *(Jeremiah 32:17)*.

> *"For with God nothing will be impossible."*
> Luke 1:37

*Read **Hebrews 11:1** and fill in the blanks.*
Now faith is the _____ of things hoped for, the _____
of things not _____.

The Greek for *substance*[34] means a standing under, and, in a technical sense, referred to a title deed. Therefore, faith is the title deed you can stand under as you wait with confident expectation for your promise from God.

When I tell one of my children that I will do something for them, they don't go around hoping that I'll be a woman of my word. They know that I will do what I say. Why? For one, I've proven myself to be faithful to them. But they also understand how much I love them and desire to do good things for them.

Our hope, or confident expectation in God, is based on the same premise. We know Him to be faithful to His Word and, experientially we know Him to be faithful based on all He has done for us in our past. I walk in great faith for God to provide for my needs because I've seen His faithful provision to meet my needs so many times and in so many different areas of my life as I've walked with Him. I also know what great love He has for me. He wants me to succeed in life. He has promised, and desires, to meet my needs. He is one hundred percent for me!

Biblical hope is more than a simple wish for something good to happen. It is a confident expectation that God will keep His promises. When we hope in God, we can have confidence that He will take care of all that concerns us. He will keep His Word. Because of this confidence, we should speak and act like it is already done.

If I'm sick in my body, for instance, I shouldn't go around telling everyone how sick I am and rehearse my symptoms to anyone who will listen. Instead, I should proclaim my faith in God to heal me based on His Scriptural promises for healing.

Faith believes God's Word over and above all other voices and all circumstances.

What is it that you need God to do in your life right now?

_____

_____

_____

*Now, please take the time to find a promise from God's Word to meet your situation. You can use a concordance (there are many on-line tools as well). Ask Holy Spirit to help you. A promise from the Word is as good as a title deed to seeing that your need is met. Write a prayer in your own words using the Scriptures that you find. (Here is an example: Father, Your Word says that by the stripes Jesus bore on His back, I am healed. Therefore, I wait with confident expectation for my healing to manifest. **Psalm 103:3** says that You heal me of all of my diseases. I don't look at my symptoms. I keep my spiritual eyes focused on Your Word.)*

_____

_____

_____

_____

_____

_____

_____

_____

_____

_____

_____

_____

_____

_____

_____

_____

Now, pray these prayers in faith until you see the promise manifested!

Day 5

Rejoicing in hope, patient in tribulation, continuing steadfastly in prayer. Romans 12:12

HELMET OF SALVATION

The Roman soldier's head and neck was protected by a helmet. It was made of bronze or iron and included two side pieces that covered and protected the cheekbones and jaw.

*Read **1 Thessalonians 5:8** and fill in the blank.*
But let us who are of the day be sober, putting on the breastplate of _____
and love, and as a helmet the _____ of salvation.

Faith and hope go hand in hand. As we learned in our last lesson, this hope is not simply wishful thinking but confidence that God will do what He says He will do.

Skandalon
"She's in so deep; she'll never get out." Lust made lewd gestures toward the others.
"Yea, she's putty in my hands." Depression never showed any emotion other than sadness, but he was excellent at what he did and a tremendous asset at furthering the kingdom of darkness. Too many children of God had fallen headlong into his clutches, being so deceived by him that many had even taken their own lives.
"Good!" Dekar clapped his hands in approval. "The prince of darkness is pleased with each of you and how well you've united in your efforts. But you must remember that he will not be completely satisfied until her life has been destroyed with no vestige of her faith left intact. You must make sure that she never turns back to Jehovah."
Page 175

Satan's first area of attack is in our mind. Specifically, he wants to bring discouragement and keep us from hoping in God. I went through a season in my life where I felt like I'd lost hope. Every day it was a struggle for me to want to remain on this earth. If not for my salvation and hope in Christ, I don't know if I'd still be here.

The irony was that it was also a time when I was seeing God's blessings flow in so many areas of my life. My first grandchild was born. I'd begun writing my book. Despite the goodness of God, Satan had convinced me that all was hopeless, and God had rejected me. It was a difficult time that has given me immense compassion for those who suffer from depression.

Depression is a very common strategy of the enemy. David, as well as Elijah, the great prophet of God, both suffered from depression and hopelessness.

Read **Romans 8:24-25** *and fill in the blanks.*
For we were saved in this _____, *but hope that is* _____
is not _____; *for why does one still hope for what he sees? But if we*
_____ *for what we do not see, we eagerly wait for it with perseverance.*

When I was going through this dark valley of depression, I had allowed Satan to get me to shift my focus from the goodness of God and onto every negative thought that bombarded my mind. And that, my friend, is his number one tactic. He wants you to be so focused on the negative arrows he shoots at you that you get your eyes off of God, and the good He has done and is doing in your life.

The Greek word for *salvation*[35] is *soteria*. It means deliverance, preservation, soundness, prosperity, happiness, rescue, and general well-being. We are not just promised these things in the sweet by-and-by. They are promises for us to declare, celebrate and enjoy today.

However, Satan will attack you and throw everything he can at you to keep you from receiving this truth. He'll gladly point out every failure and flaw in your character. His fiery darts will penetrate your mind unless you are assured of who you are and Whose you are.

Hope is said to be an anchor for our souls. It assures us of not only our salvation from the penalty of sin and death but also that we are well able to overcome the temptations of the enemy and enjoy the goodness of God as we walk out our Christian walk here on this earth (*Hebrews 6:18-19*).

Read **Romans 15:13** *and fill in the blanks.*
Now may the God of _____ *fill you with all* _____ *and*
_____ *in believing, that you may* _____ *in hope by the*
power of the Holy Spirit.

God wants us to abound in hope and has given us His Holy Spirit to enable us to do so. But we must believe without a doubt that He will fulfill His promises to us. If we choose not to believe, we will be rendered hopeless. Hope is always based on a promise. That's why it's so important to know God's promises and have them stored in your heart so that when you need them to stand on, the Holy Spirit can bring them to your remembrance.

God's desire is that we walk in the confidence and boldness of all that He has provided for us *(Proverbs 28:1)*.

The enemy knows how to twist and distort the Word of God. He will often speak just enough of the Word of God to you to confuse you and cause you to doubt what you know to be the absolute truth.

*Read **Luke 4:1-12**. Looking at verse 3 and 4, please fill in the blanks.*
And the devil _____ to Him, "_____ You are the
_____ _____ _____, command this stone to become bread."
But Jesus answered him, saying, "_____ _____ _____,
'Man shall not live by bread alone, but by every word of God.'"

Notice in *verse 4*, the devil spoke to Jesus. Now, we don't know if he manifested himself to Jesus or if Jesus only heard his voice in His inner man as we often do. The point is, Satan cast doubt on the Word of God by speaking to Jesus. He speaks to us. He can use other humans to speak his lies to us. Therefore, we want to guard against being used by him to discourage or bring pain to anyone.

Satan also attempted to get Jesus to doubt God's Word by using the conjunction *if*. We have probably all experienced the use of this word by the enemy.

If God loved you, He would have protected you.

If God cared for you, He would have kept you from getting sick.

If God is able, you'd have received the promise by now.

We have to be quick to counter the *ifs* of the enemy with the truth of God which is exactly what Christ did. His response to *if* was, *"it is written."*

I also want you to see that Satan knew Who Christ was. He knew He was the Son of God. But he attempted to get Jesus to doubt His destiny and purpose. He does the same with you and me. He wants to keep us from being all that God has called us to be and doing all that He has called us to do by getting us to doubt who we are in Christ.

Have you ever stopped to think about the thoughts you think? *Proverbs 23:7 says "For as he (a man) thinks in his heart, so is he."* Your thoughts determine who you are. Your thoughts can even determine your destiny. For instance, if Satan can convince you that you are a failure and that you'll never amount to anything, then you probably will be a failure. However, if you think about what the Word of God says about you…(*that you can do all things through*

*Christ who strengthens you according to **Philippians 4:13** and whatever you put your hands to will prosper)…then you are likely to be successful.*

Every sin begins with a thought. Anger begins with a thought. Adultery begins with a thought. No man walks out of his house and decides to have an affair that day. When we meditate continually on negative, unholy, impure thoughts, we then begin to act on what we continually think upon. For example, if I were to meditate on how offended I was by someone, I would eventually begin to talk about that offense. The best way to get over an offense is to quit thinking about it and instead, dwell on Scripture that speaks about forgiveness.

*Read **Philippians 4:8** and fill in the blanks.*
Finally, brethren, whatever things are _____, whatever things are _____, whatever things are _____, whatever things are _____, whatever things are _____, whatever things are of _____ _____, if there is any _____ and if there is anything _____ — _____ on these things.

Please close with this prayer.

Father, today I chose to think on Your goodness. I set my mind to think on those things that are true, noble, just, pure, lovely and are of a good report. I believe what Your Word says about me. I am Your child. You love me unconditionally. Help me, by the power of Your Spirit, to guard my heart and mind today and every day. In Jesus name, Amen.

5

Week Five

Skandalon Reading assignment: Chapters 17-20

Day 1

Let the word of Christ dwell in you richly in all wisdom, teaching and admonishing one another in psalms and hymns and spiritual songs, singing with grace in your hearts to the Lord.
Colossians 3:16

THE SWORD OF THE SPIRIT

*Please read **Ephesians 6:17** and fill in the blank.*
And take the helmet of salvation, and the sword of the Spirit, which is the _____ of God.

Paul used the analogy of the Roman soldier's sword to represent the Word of God. The soldier's sword was intended for close battle. It was the weapon of choice used to attack, overcome, and defeat his adversary. Every believer is called to wield the sword of the Spirit though many rarely, if ever, pick it up. Therefore, they often fall prey to the attacks of the enemy and live in a state of constant defeat.

It is interesting to note that Paul used the Greek *rhema*[36] instead of *logos* when speaking of the *Word*. A *rhema* word refers to that which is specifically spoken. It is a passage or verse that has special application to an immediate situation. As opposed to *logos*, which is the expression of a thought, a message, or a discourse. *Logos* is the message; *rhema* is the communication of the message. *Logos* is the Bible in its entirety; *rhema* is a verse from the

Bible spoken to the believer. The sword of the Spirit is the Word of God spoken to the believer as a means of combating the enemy. It originates with God, the Author, but is made alive and empowered by the Holy Spirit when spoken into the heart and mind of the believer. It is a specific word for a specific situation that you are battling in your life.

I can read the Word (*logos*) every day. However, when a passage jumps off the page and speaks directly to me, it becomes a *rhema* word. It is as if God were sitting beside me in my prayer room speaking directly to me.

When we are in the midst of a battle, we desperately need a *rhema* word from God. When the Word becomes personal to you, it is a mighty weapon in your mouth to defeat the enemy. When you wield a *rhema* word against the enemy, he cannot stand against it for long. He will eventually have to flee as long as you keep standing on the Word.

> *Now out of His mouth goes a sharp sword, that with it He should strike the nations.*
> *Revelation 19:15*

To many, the Bible is nothing more than a book that decorates a special place in their home. But for the Christian, it is our mighty weapon against a ferocious enemy who seeks to kill and destroy us. But to have faith in it being powerful enough to use in spiritual combat, we must first understand its importance.

We read in an earlier lesson, that Jesus is the living Word. The Bible refers to the Word of God as a person. Specifically, the person of Jesus Christ *(1 John 5:7)*. He was in the beginning with God. He is the Word of God.

*Read **John 1:14** and fill in the blanks.*
And the _____ became _____ and dwelt among us, and we beheld _____ glory, the glory as of the _____ _____ of the Father, full of grace and truth.

The Word became flesh! Jesus is the Word made flesh. The Bible is more than just words that are written on the pages of an ancient book. In **Revelation 19:13**, we are told that His name is called The Word (*Logos*) of God. When He speaks the Word through His servants, it becomes a sharp sword that can destroy nations and kingdoms.

*Read **2 Timothy 3:16-17** and fill in the blanks.*
_____ Scripture is given by _____ of God, and is profitable for doctrine, for reproof, for correction, for instruction in righteousness, that the man of God may be complete, thoroughly equipped for every good work.

Using the word *Scripture*[37] in the above passage, Paul was making sure that the believers understood that the New Testament was as much identified as the living voice of God as the Old Testament.

Notice that he stated, all Scripture is given by inspiration of God. This tells us that we, as humans, are not to alter the Word. It is our responsibility to study the Word to find its intended meaning and live our lives accordingly. We are warned not to add to the Word or take away from the Word *(Proverbs 30:6; Revelation 22:18)*.

> He had in His right hand seven stars, out of His mouth went a sharp two-edged sword, and His countenance was like the sun shining in its strength.
> Revelation 1:16

Many in our world today may not like or agree with the Word, but it doesn't change its validity. The Bible is our guide while here on this earth. It is a lamp to light our path in this dark world *(Psalm 119:105)* I love this acronym for BIBLE...**B**asic **I**nstructions **B**efore **L**eaving **E**arth.

> Do not add to what I command you and do not subtract from it,
> but keep the commands of the Lord your God that I give you.
> Deuteronomy 4:8

The Word of God, our sword of the Spirit, can demolish strongholds in our lives. We must be aggressive in wielding it, which means we must study the Word and have it in our heart. *Read Joshua 1:8-9 and fill in the blanks.*

This Book of the Law shall not depart from your _____, but you shall _____ in it day and night, that you may observe to _____ according to all that is written in it. For then you will make your way _____, and then you will have good _____. Have I not commanded you? Be strong and of good courage; do not be afraid, nor be dismayed, for the Lord your God is with you wherever you go."

We have a promise that when we meditate on the Word of God and keep it on our lips, we will be prosperous and successful. The Word has the power to keep us from walking in discouragement and fear. If all that were not enough, it also makes us aware that God goes with us wherever we go. Many in the body of Christ are not aware of these promises because they don't know the Word and what it promises to do for them. Therefore, they go about fighting their battles in their own strength without the realization of God's desire to take care of their every need.

Read John 6:63 and fill in the blanks.
It is the Spirit who gives _____; the flesh profits nothing. The _____ that I speak to you are _____, and they are _____.

Let's look at the word *life*[38] in this passage of Scripture. It is the Greek word *Zoe* (*sound familiar?*). It refers to the absolute fullness of life. It speaks not only of physical life but of the spiritual life that can only be obtained by faith in Jesus Christ. God's Word is life. It is life-giving and life-sustaining. The Word of God is eternal.

Read the Scriptures and match the appropriate Scripture to the correct phrase that reveals the power of God's Word.

James 1:21	*It has the power to raise the dead back to life*
Psalm 107:20	*It is illuminating in that it reveals God's will to the believer as well as shining a spotlight on our sins*
John 8:32	*The Word has the power to heal*
John 11:38-44	*It has the power to set people free from their strongholds*
Psalm 119:133	*It is Spirit-empowered and can save a man's soul from eternal death and separation from God*

With all of the power the Word of God possesses, it does us no good until we wield it as our sword. It becomes powerful in our lives when we pray it, speak it out of our mouths, and place our faith in it. A Roman soldier could carry the sharpest sword, but until he used it against his enemy, it was nothing more than a shiny weapon.

I'll never forget a vision my son had many years ago after coming home with his nose injured while at youth camp. He was tired and hurting and chose to go to bed early. About an hour after going to bed, he came into the living room and informed my husband and me that a battle was going on in his room. He said he saw an angel and a demon at war with each other. He said that every time the angel would touch the demon with his sword, he (*my son*) could breathe. However, when the angel lifted his sword, his nose was once again in pain, and he was unable to breathe.

Skandalon

One by one the negative thoughts assaulted his mind all night long. Michael tossed and turned and wrestled with the enemy praying for sleep that persistently eluded him. As soon as he would cast down one negative thought, two more would ambush his mind. By midmorning, he was mentally and physically exhausted. He sat up in bed and turned on the bedside lamp. "God, help me!" By now it was nearly four in the morning. Deuel heard the Holy Spirit speak into the spirit realm where truth speaks louder than the lies of the enemy. "My grace is sufficient for you, for My strength is made perfect in weakness." Michael suddenly remembered the scripture his dad had spoken the night before. As he began to recite it over and over to himself, he felt strength flooding into his spirit.
Pages 215

I believe God was showing us that we must wield our sword to obtain victory over our enemy. In this case, it was specifically in the area of healing. My husband, daughter and I joined my son in his room, and we all prayed together for healing for my son. The Word of God has the power to transform the heart of man. Like a sword, it can perform divine surgery; cutting skillfully into our heart to remove the sin and stains of this world.

I'd like to close today by asking God to speak His Word into our hearts. I encourage you just to sit quietly before the Lord. Ask Him to speak a rhema Word to you today. He may speak a word of healing, deliverance, or perhaps a word that brings correction. However, we can trust that when He speaks, it is always for our good. Write the word down. Meditate on the word so that it settles deep into your heart.

Father, I thank You that You are faithful to speak to Your children. Speak a rhema word to each and every person who asks of You. Speak to their situation. Speak a word of encouragement. Holy

Spirit, I ask that You would enter into our presence and speak as we seek You. Help us to quiet our souls so that we can hear from You. We love You and long to hear Your voice speaking to us. We trust that You are good and faithful. Thank You for hearing the prayers of Your children and answering our heart cries.

Day 2

But you, when you pray, go into your room, and when you have shut your door, pray to your Father who is in the secret place; and your Father who sees in secret will reward you openly. Matthew 6:6

PRAYER – ENGAGING IN THE BATTLE

There is nothing greater that anyone could do for me when I'm in the midst of a trial or need to hear from God than to pray. When someone calls or text me and tells me that God put me on their heart to pray for me, it is like receiving a precious gift. It lifts me up, gives me continued courage, and increases my faith. It reminds me that God is thinking about me.

We are to put on our spiritual armor daily. However, we step into the battle when we pray. I truly believe that it changes situations and atmospheres. I also believe that until we pray, we are opening ourselves up to be defeated by the enemy.

Prayer is more than just communication with God. It allows Him to enter into the activity of our lives and is necessary for getting our angels actively involved in our circumstances. *(Acts 12:5-12)*. But it is also a powerful weapon against our enemy. Satan hates Christians who understand the power and importance of prayer.

God's promise to every believer is that if we call out to Him in prayer, He will answer us. His answer may be *yes, no, or not at the moment* (*the dreaded wait*). His answer will only be *no* when we are not lining up our will with His or we fail to pray in faith – we'll talk about this in another lesson. However, He promises us that He hears and will answer.

Skandalon

She made it her habit to talk to the Lord as if He were in the room sitting right beside her. Rarely did a day go by when she didn't feel His presence. He was her constant companion.

Their relationship had grown over the years due to quick obedience on her part and faithfulness on His. She was familiar with His voice even when He spoke in the gentlest whisper. He'd seen her through the loss of her husband and daughter and had faithfully provided for her every need. She was never afraid of being alone because He had given His angels charge over her, and He'd promised never to leave or forsake her.

Page 90

Scripture also tells us that God can show us specific strategies as to how to do battle in any given situation. He will show us great and mighty things. He'll give us spiritual discernment as to how to pray effectively against enemy attacks.

Prayer is a means of showing God that we are dependent upon Him to meet our every need. We don't pray in order to make our needs known to God. He knows our thoughts before we even think them *(Psalm 94:11)* and our words before we are going to speak them. Therefore, we can assume He already knows our needs. Yet, He still desires that we make our requests known to Him for our sake. When He answers, we come to see how very much He loves us and desires to be involved in every aspect of our lives.

Read **1 Peter 5:6-7** and fill in the blanks.
Therefore humble yourselves under the mighty hand of God, that He may exalt you in due time,
_____ *all your care upon*
Him, for He _____
for you.

> For there is not a word on my tongue,
> But behold, O Lord, You know it altogether.
> Psalm 139:4

By prayer, we can cast all of our cares upon God demonstrating a heart that humbly trusts in His loving care, ability and desire to meet our needs.

Jesus is our greatest example of overcoming the enemy through prayer. After being baptized by John the Baptist, He was led by the Spirit into the wilderness to fast and pray for forty days. Scripture doesn't specifically say that He prayed, but we know that He used the Word to defeat every temptation brought against Him by Satan. That, in itself, is a form of prayer. After this time of fasting and prayer, He returned to Galilee in the power of the Spirit and began His three-year ministry on Earth.

> Now it came to pass in those days that He went out to the mountain to pray, and continued all night in prayer to God.
> Luke 6:12

If the Son of God received power through prayer *(Mark 1:35, Matthew 14:23, Hebrews 5:7)*, then how much more should we see the necessity of it? We read several times in the Word that He would find a quiet place to pray.

After Christ's death and resurrection, while the disciples were waiting for the promised Holy Spirit, they spent much time together in prayer *(Acts 1:12-14)*. The early church was built on a foundation of prayer. The apostles gave themselves continually to prayer and the ministry of the Word *(Acts 6:4)*. Every time the enemy attacked the early church, they turned to God in prayer, seeking His deliverance and guidance.

There is nothing impossible with God and nothing too difficult for Him. Therefore, we can bring every request to Him, no matter how large or small. Let's look at answers to some seemingly impossible prayers in the Word.

*Read **Joshua 10:12-14**. What did Joshua ask of God and what was the result of his prayer?*

_____

_____

_____

*Read **1 Kings 17:17-24**. What happened when Elijah cried out to God for the life of the widow's dead son?*

_____

_____

_____

*Read **Isaiah 38:1-9**. Hezekiah was sick and dying. Though God had sent the prophet Isaiah to tell him that he was going to die, Hezekiah prayed. What was the result of his prayer? How did God assure him that his prayer would be answered?*

_____

_____

_____

*Read **Acts 12:5-14**. What happened as a result of the disciples gathering in prayer for Peter's release from prison?*

_____

_____

_____

How has God answered your prayer request to a situation that seemed impossible without His divine intervention? _____

_____

_____

_____

I remember once when my family needed a new washing machine. My husband told me I could go purchase a new washer on credit since it was something we considered to be a necessity. We didn't have the money to spend on a washer at the time. The Lord spoke to me and told me that I could go charge it but that if I would wait on Him, He would provide. Now, I must add, I knew that if I waited on the Lord I might end up at the corner laundromat. I hated having to go to the laundromat. However, I took up the challenge. Two weeks passed by. One morning I received a phone call from a woman at our local appliance store. She asked me if I wanted my washing machine in white or almond. I was stunned. She couldn't reveal who was purchasing the machine for me. However, she told me that a brand new washer was going to be delivered to my home that day. God did what He had promised to do. For me, it was an answer to prayer that I have never forgotten.

I've learned over the years to bring every request to God. It doesn't matter how big or how small that request is. If something is important to me, it's important to my Father. Before my husband and I were to get married, I desperately wanted a bottle of perfume that cost way more than my budget would allow (*I wanted to smell nice on my honeymoon*). To me, it seemed like too small a thing to bother God about (*I mean, He's pretty busy, right?*). I was walking from the parking garage to go into my office and thought, *I wish I had perfume for my honeymoon*. As soon as I got to my desk the phone rang. It was a dear friend. She said God had laid it on her heart to get me perfume for my wedding day and wanted to be sure she knew exactly what brand I used. I knew God was demonstrating to me the desire to meet all of my needs and give me the desires of my heart as well.

In *Ephesians 6:18*, we are commanded to '*pray always.*' I know that there are some new sleep-deprived mommies that consider it a challenge to spend fifteen minutes a day in prayer. Others are overwhelmed with the responsibility of getting children ready for school before heading off to a busy day at work and then faced with homework, dinner and family time at the end of the day. So, how can we possibly find the time to pray?

We can lead very busy lives without short-changing our time with the Lord. Personally, I couldn't live without starting my day with prayer. However, my prayer life has evolved over the years. When I first came to understand the importance of prayer, I was a single mom of two small children with a very demanding job. I tried getting up early in the morning before my children were awake only to find myself too sleepy to pray. However, I had a thirty-minute drive to and from work and learned to use that time to fellowship with the Lord.

After I married my husband and became a stay-at-home mom, I would get up early and pray before homeschooling my children. Often, I would stay up after everyone had gone to bed and have a quiet time. I grew to love and depend on my time spent in His presence.

But, I've also learned the joy of praying always, or to pray without ceasing, as Paul tells us to do in *1 Thessalonians 5:17*. When a need comes to mind, I pray. When I see a wreck on the freeway, I pray for those involved as well as those who might find out that their loved one has passed. I'm often led to pray for the needs I see in the lives of those on the news or social media.

Praying always isn't necessarily about petitioning God for the needs of others or myself. It can also be a prayer of thanksgiving for a beautiful sunset or perhaps a desperate cry for help. And sometimes, when I feel overwhelmed, it might just be a whisper of His name. *Jesus!*

Praying always is simply bringing Jesus into every moment of our lives. It is a realization that He is with you, wants to direct you, instruct you, and enable you as you go through your day.

*Read **Psalm 55:17**. Considering the fact that David was a king, we can probably safely assume he was a pretty busy guy. When did he find time to pray?* _____

*Read **Luke 18:1** and fill in the blank.*
Then He spoke a parable to them, that men _____ *ought to pray and not lose heart.*

Think about ways you can incorporate prayer into your daily life. Can you have a quiet time in the morning or perhaps at night after everyone is in bed? Do you need to set your clock to remind you to get up early in the morning for prayer? Maybe you need to put a sticky note in your car reminding you to pray while you drive to work?

Habakkuk 2:2 instructs us to write the vision so that we can run with it. You'll never get started without a plan.

Write out a plan and ask God for grace to run with it!

_____
_____
_____
_____
_____
_____
_____
_____
_____
_____
_____
_____

Let's close out today with a prayer!

Father, help me to see the importance of prayer. Take me deeper in my prayer life. Teach me to pray always bringing every request, no matter how large or small, to You. Holy Spirit, lay the needs of others upon my heart so that I can intercede for them. I want my love toward You as well as others to grow as I spend time in prayer. Draw me into a deeper fellowship with You as I pray. Let prayer become a discipline in my life that I cannot live without any more than I can live without breathing. I'll not be condemned on the days I fail to spend time in Your presence because prayer is about our love relationship toward each other. Most of all, remind me daily that You, the Creator of heaven and earth, long to spend time alone with me. I am overwhelmed that You would desire time with me. Enable me to long for Your presence just as You long for mine. In Jesus name, Amen!

Day 3

"So I say to you, ask, and it will be given to you; seek, and you will find; knock, and it will be opened to you. For everyone who asks receives, and he who seeks finds, and to him who knocks it will be opened." Luke 11:9-10

PRAYER – DON'T GIVE UP UNTIL THE DEVIL DEPARTS

Read **Colossians 4:2** *and fill in the blanks.*
_____ *earnestly in prayer, being* _____
in it with thanksgiving…

The Apostle Paul instructs the believer to continue in prayer (*praying always!*) and to be vigilant about prayer. The word *vigilant*[39] means to be carefully noticing problems or signs of danger; alertly watchful especially to avoid danger. Through prayer we are made aware of the schemes and traps of the enemy, we become more sensitive as the Spirit alerts us, and can be instructed as to how to pray effectively to counter an attack. God can give us divine strategies so that we see our circumstances change.

I recall a struggle that my husband and I were having early on in our marriage, regarding the discipline of my son. I would cry, threaten, nag, and use any other means necessary to get him to change. I felt like he often disciplined harshly, laying down rules that were birthed out of legalism instead of love. My children were not his by birth. Therefore, I felt like he was particularly hard on my son. One day while praying about it, I asked God when He was going to intervene. He pretty much told me that He would change my situation when I quit trying to change my husband (*ouch!*). Sure enough, when I learned to keep quiet, my husband started developing a more tender heart toward my son. God has completely healed their relationship, and they are much closer now.

We have already established that we have a very real enemy whose name is Satan. His goal is to destroy the life of every believer in Christ. When we are vigilant in our prayer life, we can discover his plans, pray against them, and live victoriously. The more vigilant we are, the more victorious our walk with Christ will be. Another translation for *vigilant*[40] is the word *watch*. We can get a greater understanding of the meaning by looking at the Greek definition of the word: to take heed lest through remission and indolence some destructive calamity suddenly overtakes one. When we fail to be watchful through prayer, the enemy can overtake us. Isn't this what happened to Zoe, the main character of our story?

Knowing that we have an enemy should make us aware of the need to be watchful for his attack at all times. Peter tells us that Satan is like a roaring lion. There are several characteristics of a lion that I would liken to Satan. A lion will ambush his victim through the element of surprise. He is stealthy, aggressive and ruthless. Once a lion has a victim in his grasp, he is hell-bent (*no pun intended!*) on devouring it.

Not only are we instructed to be vigilant but also we are to continue earnestly in prayer. I once heard it said that we are not to give up until we see the devil depart. I think that's what Paul meant when he told us to continue earnestly in prayer.

Many never see the answer to their prayers because they give up before they see the answer appear. We cannot grow weary in our prayer life simply because we don't see the Lord answering our prayers within our time frame. God operates outside of time, and our earthly time constraints do not limit Him. What might seem to take forever to us is equivalent to the blink of an eye to God.

*Read **Galatians 6:9** and fill in the blanks.*
And let us not _____ _____ while doing good, for in _____ _____ we shall reap if we do not _____ _____.

Skandalon

Jasiel held Amos in place just before the entrance to his wife's prayer closet. Barbara had been praying fervently for Amos since she'd come to know the Lord. Because of her deep love for God and appreciation of all He'd done for her, she'd grown quickly in her faith and desperately wanted her husband to become a Christian too. She longed for the day when she could share her faith and love for God with him.
God had heard her cries and seen her tears and was intervening on her behalf. He'd also heard the prayers of Abby, Zoe's grandma. She loved him like her very own son and also never failed, night and day, to bring his name up to the Lord for salvation.
Page 160-161

My husband loves to grow things. At this moment, I have a red solo cup bearing precious seeds sitting on my dining room table. No doubt, he'll plant them as soon as he gets the chance.

Before planting his seeds, he will have to find the perfect dirt (*my husband loves good dirt!*). He has been known to go collect cow patties from a friend's pasture (*I know…gross!*) so that he can mix them in with the soil to get the maximum potential to grow healthy plants.

He plants the seed, waters it, places the plant where it will receive the proper amount of sunshine, and then the waiting period begins. He'll check on his plant every day. Now, on the first day after planting, he doesn't pull out his seed to check on it simply because he sees no new growth. He's a gardener. He knows that if he did that, he stands the chance of destroying his seed.

However, that is what we often do when we are praying for a situation. We don't see the answer to our prayer directly after praying so we, in essence, pull up our seed. We give up before the need is met. God has an answer on the way, but we forfeit the answer because of a lack of patience. We grow weary because we think it's taking too long and therefore, surmise it must not be God's will to answer our prayer.

Even after the first week, my husband continues patiently to monitor his plant. He checks on it daily with the expectation of seeing fruit come forth. He has faith that because the conditions are right for his plant to grow…good soil, water, and sunshine…he will eventually see a shoot sticking out of the soil.

Read Luke 11:5-8 and Luke 18:1-8. What is the common theme within these two passages of Scripture? _____

_____

_____

Both of these parables have a common meaning. They teach us about persistence in our faith and being unceasing in our prayer life. The judge in this second parable neither feared God nor did he have respect or consideration for man, yet because this widow persisted to go before him time after time, he gave in to her demand. Since we have a compassionate, loving God…we can come persistently and boldly before the throne of grace to see our needs met, with confidence that our God hears us and will answer.

The Greek word translated as *weary*[41] in *Luke 18:5* is the imagery of a boxer beating his opponent black and blue. It refers to the part of the face that is under the eyes. This heathen judge is basically saying that he is afraid of not giving the persistent widow what she wants otherwise she may end up beating him up and giving him a black eye in the process! When we continually go to God with our case….we give the enemy a black eye!

According to Webster's, the word *persist*[42] means– to take a stand; stand firm; to refuse to give up especially when faced with opposition or difficulty; to be insistent in the repetition or pressing of an utterance.

Jesus, through these two parables, is encouraging us as believers not to give up in our continual coming to God with our requests. The widow didn't say to herself, "Well, that judge is mean, he hates everyone, he's not going to give me justice so I'll have to take justice into my own hands." She just kept going back...again and again.

Think of a time when you gave up or quit praying for the salvation of a loved one because you didn't see the results you wanted in your timing? _____ _____

_____

_____

Have you ever had a prayer request that you did not see answered in your timing? _____

Did you try to fulfill the need on your own instead of waiting on God? (For example...did you quit a job instead of waiting on God to change your boss's heart? Did you borrow money for a large purchase because you didn't think God was going to provide?) If yes, please explain. _____

_____

_____

_____

_____

_____

Persistence[43] in prayer can also be translated as over-boldness or shamelessness. God is looking for bold, persistent and even shameless faith. Though others may think you should give up asking, standing and believing...God says, *Persist!* He is looking for those who will pray and not give up!

Everything that you need from God will only come when you pray to Him and ask Him for it. It's His way of demonstrating to us that He alone is our Father who will supply all of our needs.

The word *supplication*[44] in **Philippians 4:6,** suggests intense, earnest prayer for an extended amount of time. In supplication, it is not that our many words or extended amount of time in prayer move God to answer our request. Rather, our crying out to Him is a demonstration of our complete humility and dependency upon Him and a transference of the burden into His hands.

*Read **Daniel 10:12-13** and answer the following questions.*
According to Michael, one of the chief princes (angelic beings), when was Daniel's prayer heard?

_____

_____

Why was there a delay in the answer getting to Daniel? How long was the delay?

_____

_____

_____

We can certainly conclude from this passage of Scripture that the enemy will hinder God's answer from coming forth. He will do all that he can to convince you to give up. For this reason, we must persist in our prayers. We never know when the answer will come. I believe that it is safe to say the more the need impacts the kingdom…the greater the resistance the enemy will bring.

> Be anxious for nothing, but in everything by prayer and supplication, with thanksgiving, let your requests be made known to God.
> Philippians 4:6

I want to leave you today with *James 5:16* in the Amplified version.

Confess to one another therefore your faults (your slips, your false steps, your offenses, your sins) and pray [also] for one another, that you may be healed and restored [to a spiritual tone of mind and heart]. The earnest (heartfelt, continued) prayer of a righteous man makes tremendous power available [dynamic in its working].

The Word tells us to be unceasing in prayer…keep pressing, don't give up, don't let up. *Don't give up until you see the devil leave, and the kingdom come!*

Day 4

For indeed the gospel was preached to us as well as to them; but the word which they heard did not profit them, not being mixed with faith in those who heard it. Hebrews 4:2

THE PRAYER OF FAITH

We've discussed faith as well as prayer in other lessons. But I'd like to explore a type of prayer we don't often hear about in the church. I want to talk about the prayer of faith or the prayer that changes circumstances and situations. This type of prayer witnesses mountains moving and miracles occurring.

I believe that one reason many of us lack a persevering spirit in prayer and, therefore, go without our prayers being answered is that we do not mix our prayers with faith.

Read James 5:13-18. Look at verse 15 and fill in the blanks.
And the _____ _____ _____ *will save the sick, and the Lord will raise him up. And if he has committed sins, he will be forgiven.*

What is the prayer of faith that James was speaking of in this passage? I can assure you of this…it's not a magic prayer. Nor is it prayer built around a formula. Many would argue that every prayer is a prayer of faith. *Really?* Have you ever prayed a prayer with the tag line, "*If it is Your will?*" That would *not* have been a prayer of faith.

> *Yet it pleased the Lord to bruise Him; He has put Him to grief. When You make His soul an offering for sin...*
> *Isaiah 53:10*

Read Matthew 26:36-39. We see in this passage of Scripture that Jesus' soul was sorrowful, even to death. So much so that His sweat became like drops of blood. It wasn't that He feared death. He had never sinned nor experienced separation from the Father. He knew that the time was upon Him to carry upon himself every single sin that humanity had ever committed, or would ever commit. Knowing that the Father could not be in the presence of sin and that sin brings separation from God, He was acutely aware that to carry the sins of the world would require a time of separation from the Father (*Matthew 27:46, Psalm 22:1*).

Make no mistake; Jesus knew all along His purpose upon this Earth. He understood and was zealous to do the will of His Father *(John 5:30)*. Look at *Acts 2:23* in the Amplified version.

*This Jesus, when delivered up according to the definite and fixed purpose
and settled plan and foreknowledge of God, you crucified and put out of the way
[killing Him] by the hands of lawless and wicked men.*

If Jesus had *not* been aware of the will of the Father and the purpose for His life here on this Earth, why would He have cried out, "*It is finished!*" just before He died? He'd known the will of the Father from the foundation of this world (*1 Peter 1:20*).

If He knew the will of the Father, why did He pray in the Garden, "*Nevertheless, not as I will, but as You will?*" It was a prayer of surrender to the Father. Having battled with His soul, He came to the place of complete surrender. When Jesus prayed those words, He was declaring Himself to be completely submitted to the will of His Father.

> *All who dwell on the earth will worship him, whose names have not been written in the Book of Life of the Lamb slain from the foundation of the world.*
> Revelation 13:8

When we attach the words, *if it is Your will,* to our prayer, it is to be a demonstration of a surrendered heart to the will of the Father. You might pray this prayer when you are not sure exactly what the will of God is for your situation. For example, let's say you are thinking about changing jobs, and you're not sure if it's the will of God. You might ask God if it is His will for you to take a new position. Your heart, in that prayer, is to surrender to His will.

It is not something we would pray, however, when praying the prayer of faith. When praying the prayer of faith, we must base our prayers on the will of the Father that we already know. How do we find out the will of the Father? Through the Word of God. When we are praying the prayer of faith, we are praying for what God the Father already desires to give us according to His Word.

When a prayer is based on the Word of God (*which is the will of God*), we can have confidence that our prayer will be answered.

Read 1 John 5:14-15 and fill in the blanks.
Now this is the _____ that we have in Him, that if we ask
anything according to _____ _____, He hears us. And if we know
that _____ _____ _____, whatever we ask, we know that we
_____ _____ _____ that we have asked of
Him.

131

We can have confidence that our prayers will be answered when we ask according to the will of God. Therefore, it's important to know the Word so that we can discern God's will for our life.

God has made His will very clear to us in the Word. We can study the life of Christ to know and understand the will of the Father *(John 4:34, John 6:38-39)*. He did what He saw the Father doing and spoke the heart of the Father. Therefore, if Jesus healed, we can rightly assume it is the Father's will to heal. If Jesus delivered those who were oppressed of the devil; it is the Father's will to bring deliverance to the captives. Obviously, it is Jesus' will to forgive because He taught forgiveness.

Look at *John 10:10* in the Amplified version.

> *The thief comes only in order to steal and kill and destroy. I came that they may have and enjoy life, and have it in abundance (to the full, till it overflows).*

The word *abundance"* is the Greek word *perissos*. It means superabundance, excessive, overflowing, surplus, over and above, more than enough, profuse, extraordinary, above the ordinary, and more than sufficient.

We can know with assurance that it is God's will to give us an abundant life, and, therefore, pray the prayer of faith for an abundant life. Please note, however, this does not mean we'll never face trials or distressing situations.

We can pray in faith for peace because Christ is the Prince of Peace *(Isaiah 9:6)*.

We can pray in faith for wisdom and guidance because we know, based on the Word, that it is God's will to give us wisdom and to guide us in all matters.

Have you ever finished out a prayer for the salvation of a loved one with the words, *if it be Your will?* I would hope not! Because we know that Jesus came to the earth to bring salvation. We know it is His will to save, therefore, when we pray for the salvation of a lost soul, we pray with confidence *(or, we certainly should)*.

Read Mark 11:22-24 and fill in the blanks.

So Jesus answered and said to them, "Have _____ in God. For assuredly, I say to you, whoever _____ to this mountain, 'Be removed and be cast into the sea,' and does not _____ in his heart, but _____ that those things he_____ will be done, he _____ have _____ he _____.

Therefore I say to you, _____ things you ask when you pray, _____ that you _____ them, and you _____ have them.

We can glean several things from this powerful verse.

First off, in order to pray, we must have faith in God. Having faith in God means we must have faith that He keeps His Word *(Hebrews 6:13-19)*, that He loves us and desires to do good for us *(Jeremiah 29:11)*, and that nothing is impossible with Him.

*Read **Hebrews 11:6** and fill in the blanks.*
But without faith it is _____ to please Him...
The Bible states that when we come to God we must _____ that He is God
and that He _____ _____ _____ of those who diligently
seek Him.

To receive the answer to our prayers, we must have a firm belief that He desires to reward us. In other words, we are to believe when we ask according to the will of God that the answer is yes, and the answer is on its way!

Second, there is no room for doubt in the prayer of faith. Once you lay hold of the promise of God, you hold onto it until you see the answer come forth. You persevere in faith.

*Read **James 1:6-7** and fill in the blanks.*
But let him ask in _____, with no _____, for he
who doubts is like a wave of the sea driven and tossed by the wind. For let not that man suppose
that he will _____ _____ from the Lord;

This Scripture makes it clear that when we doubt we will not receive anything from the Lord. It renders our prayers ineffective (*sorry, that's not my word but the Word of God*). When you doubt, you do without! Fear and doubt feed off of each other. The enemy will always try to convince you to doubt that God can and will answer your prayers (*and, he'll often use humans to do so*).

> "And in that day you will ask Me nothing. Most assuredly, I say to you, whatever you ask the Father in My name He will give you. Until now you have asked nothing in My name. Ask, and you will receive, that your joy may be full."
> John 16:23-24

The third lesson we learn from *Mark 11:22-24*, is that we have what we say! What we believe with our heart, we will confess from our lips. Confession is important. It is coming into agreement with the will of God. Faith is released when we speak. However, our faith must be based securely on the Word and will of God. Speaking in faith releases God's Word of promise into your situation (we'll *study more on this powerful spiritual principle in Week Eight*).

*Look at **Matthew 17:20** and fill in the blank.*
So Jesus said to them, "Because of your unbelief; for assuredly, I say to you, if you have faith as a mustard seed, you will _____ to this mountain, 'Move from here to there,' and it will move; and _____ _____ _____ _____ for you.

In the above passage, Jesus was speaking to His disciples. They'd tried unsuccessfully to heal a boy who was suffering from epileptic seizures. Before giving His disciples a dissertation regarding mountain-moving faith, Jesus rebuked them.

Notice that He told them that they had to say to the mountain…move. In other words, He didn't say look at the mountain or just think about the mountain and it will move. He didn't tell them to meditate real hard on the mountain to get it to move, and they certainly weren't instructed to hope that the mountain would move. No, He told them that they must speak to the mountain for the mountain to move.

The key to the prayer of faith is speaking the Word of God over your situation. If you are in need of healing, find Scriptures that pertain to healing and pray those Scriptures every day. The Bible says that faith comes by hearing and hearing by the Word of God. Speak the Word of God to your mountain!

The Word tells us that we are to call those things that are not as though they were *(Romans 4:17)*. The prayer of faith speaks faith over the situation even when the answer is not yet seen in the natural.

Please don't think you have to get in bondage to your words. I've seen and heard people get pretty crazy with this scriptural principle. If you are sick, you don't have to lie and say, *"No, I'm not sick."* What you are to do is confess God's Word over your body. If someone asks you if you are sick, you can say something like this, '*Yes I am, but I believe God's Word that says I am healed*.'

The prayer of faith is founded on the name of Jesus. *Read **John 14:13-14** and fill in the blank.*
And whatever you ask in _____ _____, that I will do, that the Father may be glorified in the Son. If you ask anything in _____ _____, I will do it.

When we pray in the name of Jesus, we are praying the will of God. We are asking in the authority of His name to promote His kingdom interest and agenda.

When one has been given the power of attorney for someone else, they have the legal authority to make important decisions, sign legal documentation, and act in that person's best interest. When we pray in the name of Jesus, we are praying as one who has been given the power of attorney by the King of Kings. Therefore, He backs up what we pray when it is in line with His will.

Look at *2 Corinthians 5:20* in the Amplified version.

So we are Christ's ambassadors, God making His appeal as it were through us. We [as Christ's personal representatives] beg you for His sake to lay hold of the divine favor [now offered you] and be reconciled to God.

Skandalon

He then prayed the prayer out loud and followed up with his own words to the Father. "Thank You, Father, that You are giving me a faith vision for my wife. Thank You that You can and will take all of this devastating loss in her life to draw her into a deep, abiding relationship with You. Thank You that her faith will be deepened by this tremendous trial she is walking through. I will stand in faith with You and pray for her eyes to be opened and her ears to hear Your voice saying to her, 'This is the way, walk in it.' I thank You for the day that she will be able to look back on her life and count all the things that she has lost as nothing in comparison to the future she has with You. I know the day is coming when You will restore to her the joy of her salvation. I praise You for speaking to me today and giving me a fresh hope for Zoe.
In Jesus' name."
Page 234

When we pray in the name of Jesus, we are praying just as He would pray. Our prayers must be free from selfish motives or misguided desires.

Is there something you've been praying for but have yet to see come to pass? Pray the prayer of faith over this desire and back your prayer up with the Word of God. Write it down. Lay hold of the promise of God. Pray with boldness and faith. Confess that your prayer is already answered and speak as if it were already done!

_____

_____

_____

Now thank the Lord daily that you have what you have asked for! Be blessed.

Day 5

Giving thanks always for all things to God the Father in the name of our Lord Jesus Christ...
Ephesians 5:20

PRAISE AND WORSHIP IN WARFARE

I once read that *"God intends for the hammer blows of life to bend our wings upward into a position of constant praise. He wants to bring us to the place where our fixed attitude to each challenge is "in everything give thanks[46].""*

Praise and worship are not just about singing songs along with the worship team on Sunday morning. Praise and worship can be a powerful weapon wielded against our enemy.

Read Acts 16:16-34 and answer the following questions. At what time of the day were Paul and Silas praying and singing hymns to God? _____
_____

Where were they during this time of worship? _____

What was the result of their worship? _____
_____
_____

I hope that somewhere within your answer you noted that the prison doors were opened, all of the prisoner's chains were loosed, and the jailer and his household received salvation as a consequence of these men praising in the midst of tragic circumstances.

Praise that springs forth from the heart can break even the strongest chains of bondage. It's important to note that Paul and Silas were imprisoned for their faith in Christ. They were following the Holy Spirit and doing the work of the Lord, yet they ran into adverse circumstances. Even when we are doing everything that God has directed us to do, we can still find ourselves in the midst of an attack of the enemy. However, if you want to shake things up, see doors open, and have your chains break in two, begin to praise God in spite of what you are facing.

When we choose the pathway of prayer and praise, we will always see victory. I'll never forget a time in my life when I was going through a particular trial. I'd just received some devastating news before driving to work. I was crying out to the Lord in my car asking Him what He wanted me to do. Suddenly, my eyes were drawn to a bumper sticker on the car in front of me. It read: *rejoice, pray, give thanks!*

God's will for every believer is that we will rejoice in every situation.

Read James 1:2-4 and fill in the blanks.
My brethren, count it all _____ when you fall into various _____, knowing that the testing of your faith produces patience. But let patience have its perfect work, that you may be perfect and complete, lacking nothing.

Notice that Paul and Silas began to pray and praise at midnight. Midnight represents the darkest hour; a time when our situation looks overwhelmingly impossible. I'm sure the enemy thought he'd won. He'd orchestrated this imprisonment to dishearten and silence these men of God as well as the early church. But he hadn't counted on them shaking their prison

> *Rejoice always,*
> *Pray without ceasing,*
> *In everything give thanks: for this is the will of God in Christ Jesus for you.*
> *1 Thessalonians 5:16-18*

bonds loose through the power of praise. At midnight, they invited God into the midst of their prison, and a mighty earthquake opened the doors of every cell.

Midnight is the time when we have to choose between being pitiful or powerful. We can cry, moan and groan about our circumstances or we can praise the God who is in control of everything that happens in our life.

Satan desires that we despair, lose hope, doubt the love and faithfulness of our God, and complain when we find ourselves trapped in his schemes. He uses oppression and difficulties to convince us to turn our eyes away from Christ and onto our circumstances. Paul and Silas knew that their Savior was well able to deliver them. They demonstrated their trust in Him when they praised Him.

When we praise God while going through the trials and tribulations of life, it is a demonstration to Him of our absolute trust in His ability to meet every need and take care of everything that concerns us. This type of praise is referred to as the sacrifice of praise. It is powerful!

It is praise offered when you receive the cancer diagnosis from your doctor. It's the sacrificial praise offered up to God when there are more days of the month left than there is money in your bank account. When it appears that your children or your spouse will never turn to

God, it's a sweet smelling offer of praise to God that declares to Him as well as your enemy that you know God is able in spite of how the situation appears in the natural.

*Read **Hebrews 13:15** and fill in the blank.*
Therefore by Him let us continually offer the _____ *of* _____ *to God, that is, the fruit of our lips, giving* _____ *to His name.*

The word *sacrifice*[47] is the Greek word *thusia* and comes from the root *thuo*, which means to kill or slaughter for a purpose. A sacrifice of praise often means that we must slaughter our fear, our desire for things to go our way, self-pity, lack of trust, or anything that would cause our focus to be turned away from Christ. Praise reminds us that He is worthy and able to overcome the circumstances we find ourselves walking through. It centers us in Him and His will for our lives. It reaffirms our trust in Him, in His faithfulness and love.

When we think of the word *sacrifice*, we often think of an inconvenience or the giving of a costly gift. However, in the Hebrew language, it involves the offering of an innocent life. The more your praise costs you…the more it will pay off.

Look at *Psalm 8:2* in the New International version.

Through the praise of children and infants you have established a stronghold against your enemies, to silence the foe and the avenger.

Now, please look up this Scripture in the New King James version of the Bible and fill in the blanks.

Out of the mouth of babes and nursing infants You have ordained _____ , *because of Your enemies, that You may* _____ *the enemy and the avenger.*

Jesus quoted a portion of this verse in *Matthew 21:15-16. Please look up this passage and fill in the blank.*
But when the chief priests and scribes saw the wonderful things that He did, and the children crying out in the temple and saying, "Hosanna to the Son of David!" they were indignant and said to Him, "Do You hear what these are saying?"
And Jesus said to them, "Yes. Have you never read, 'Out of the mouth of babes and nursing infants You have perfected _____ '?"*

There is a strength that comes upon the believer when he or she will turn to God in praise. This word *strength* is the same word translated as *might* used of David when he danced and praised the Lord while bringing the ark of the Lord into the City of David. When you choose praise over pity, God will strengthen you to walk through the battle!

I've heard it said that Corrie and Betsie ten Boom while imprisoned in a concentration camp during the reign of Hitler in Germany, learned to praise God in

> *Then David danced before the Lord with all his might; and David was wearing a linen ephod.*
> *2 Samuel 6:14*

the midst of a bunkhouse infested with fleas. They soon realized that the fleas for which they thanked God were the very thing that kept their prison guards out of their barracks. This enabled them to read their Bible and freely share the Gospel with the other prisoners.

Skandalon

He had sent one of his most trusted servants, Bithron, well known for living up to his name, which means divisions, to head up the attack. He'd given him specific orders: use Gossip, Backbiting, Murmuring, and Complaining to wear down the saints of New Zion Fellowship when this sin is exposed and sow mistrust of the pastor into the hearts of his parishioners.

What he hadn't counted on was the pastor being a man of great integrity and faith, given to mercy and compassion, leading the church into a time of intercession for the perpetrator and his victim. He cringed as they cried out for the complete restoration of the young man and healing for the young girl he'd molested. And to make matters worse, after they'd spent time in prayer that morning, they penetrated his kingdom of darkness giving angels even more power to defend against his forces as they wholeheartedly dived into triumphant worship of Jehovah singing songs of deliverance and victory.

Page 210

God can turn our situation around for good when we praise Him through it.

In the book of Habakkuk is a song of faith that Habakkuk prayed to the Lord. It was his act of praise at a time when He could not see the hand of God moving to deliver him. It was a declaration of faith before he could see the victory with his natural eyes.

*Read **Habakkuk 3:17-19** and fill in the blanks.*
Though the fig tree may not blossom, nor fruit be on the vines; though the labor of the olive may fail, and the fields yield no food; though the flock may be cut off from the fold, and there be no herd in the stalls— Yet I will _____ in the Lord, I will _____ in

the God of my salvation. The Lord God is my strength; _____ _____ *make my feet like deer's feet, And* _____ _____ *make me walk on my high hills.*

There have been many times when I've prayed this song of faith to God. In modern day language, my prayer might go something like this:

Though there is not enough money in the bank account and I don't see any coming from any other source; though my children are not walking with the Lord; though the ministry doors I've prayed for to open remain shut, and though I battle with disease…yet, I will rejoice in the Lord; I will joy in the God of my salvation.

Though this song was written at a very difficult time in Habakkuk's life, he made the choice to sing a song of worship and praise to God. Worship is a choice we have to make. God will not force us to worship. However, I can promise you that the devil trembles when you choose to worship in the midst of the storms of life.

Praise brings God into the midst of your circumstances.

Read **Psalm 22:3-4** *and fill in the blanks.*
But You are holy, _____ *in the* _____ *of Israel.*
Our fathers _____ *in You; they* _____ ,
and You _____ *them.*

The word *enthroned*[48] is translated as *dwell* in the Amplified version. It means to sit down, to remain, to settle, or marry. God's presence comes to sit down in the midst of us as well as our situation when we praise Him. His power is manifested where His presence dwells. Where God takes up residence, the devil has to leave.

Read **Psalm 27:6** *and fill in the blanks.*
And now shall my head be lifted up above my _____ *all around me;*
Therefore I will offer _____ *of* _____ *in His tabernacle; I will*
sing, yes, I will sing _____ *to the Lord.*

As I shared in an earlier lesson, I went through a season of deep, dark depression in my life. I had to learn to live this Scripture. My very survival came to depend on me choosing to praise God and choosing joy each and every day.

I'm going to ask you to take a passage of Scripture (*like* **Habakkuk 3:17-19**) and make it a personal song of praise to the Lord. It doesn't have to be that Scripture. You may have one that is closer to your heart. I'll give you an example:

Lord, I do not fear because I know that You are always with me. I refuse to be discouraged or dismayed because You are my God and You never leave me alone or abandon me. In the midst of my trial, You will strengthen me and help me. You will uphold me with Your righteous right hand. Therefore, in faith, I praise You and worship You and wait for Your deliverance.

6

Week Six

Skandalon Reading assignment: Chapters 21-24

Day 1

For our gospel did not come to you in word only, but also in power, and in the Holy Spirit and in much assurance, as you know what kind of men we were among you for your sake.
1 Thessalonians 1:5

AIR SUPPORT IN WARFARE

We've been learning about spiritual warfare and the importance of prayer. This week, I want to discuss the Holy Spirit and His role in making us overcomers in the midst of battle. I can't even begin to imagine a day of my life without Him. Certainly, I wouldn't make it through a trial without His wisdom, insight, presence, and protection.

It astounds me that many in the church today do not understand the role of the Holy Spirit in their lives. Knowing Him is vital to the spiritual growth of the believer. We can't possibly walk out our faith in Christ without Him.

The Holy Spirit is not some vague, impersonal force. On the contrary, He is equal in every way with God the Father and God the Son. He is the third person of the Trinity. He was, or existed, in the beginning, and played a role in creation.

*Read **Genesis 1:1-2** and fill in the blanks.*
In the beginning _____ created the heavens and the earth. The earth was without form, and void; and darkness was on the face of the deep. And the _____

of God was hovering over the face of the waters.

The word *God*[49] is the Hebrew word *Elohim*, which is the plural form. It reveals to us that God is a three-part being. Elohim speaks of God in His fullness. When we see the word Elohim, it refers to God as Creator. Therefore, we know that the Holy Spirit was not only present but actively involved in Creation. Each member of the Trinity has a specific function though they are coequal. I once heard a teaching that clarified their roles like this: The Father is the Executive, The Son is the Architect, and the Holy Spirit is the Contractor.[50]

We see evidence of the Father, Son, and Holy Spirit all mentioned in one verse. The Three working in perfect harmony together.

*Read **Luke 3:21-23** and answer the following questions.*
In this passage, who is being baptized? _____

Who descended upon Jesus in bodily form like a dove? _____

Who spoke from heaven saying, "You are My beloved Son; in You I am well pleased."? _____
_____

We often hear of the Holy Spirit referred to as a person, or as having very personal qualities. He is never referred to in Scripture as *It,* therefore we shouldn't refer to Him as *It* either. He is a person and desires a relationship with each one of us.

*Read **John 14:16-18** and fill in the blanks.*
And I will pray the Father, and He will give you another _____,
that _____ *may abide with you forever— the* _____ *of*
truth, whom the world cannot receive, because it neither sees _____ *nor knows*
_____*; but you know* _____*, for* _____ *dwells with you*
and will be in you. I will not leave you orphans; I will come to you.

Jesus refers to the Holy Spirit, whom He declares the Father will send in His place, as *He.* A distinct person!

The word *another*[51] is a word that means one besides, another of the same kind. Jesus was declaring that the role of the Holy Spirit would be different, yet He would continue the work that Jesus had begun in the life of the disciples.

Let's look at some of the attributes that make Him a definite personality.

The Holy Spirit has intellect, or the ability to think logically.

Look at *Romans 8:27* in the Amplified version.

And He Who searches the hearts of men knows what is in the mind of the [Holy] Spirit [what His intent is] because the Spirit intercedes and pleads [before God] in behalf of the saints according to and in harmony with God's will.

You will also note from the above Scripture, that the Holy Spirit intercedes for the saints of God in harmony with the will of God. Everything He does lines up with the will of the Father.

He has emotions and can be grieved.

*Look at **Ephesians 4:30** and fill in the blank.*
And do not _____ *the Holy Spirit of God, by whom you were sealed for the day of redemption.*

The word *grieve*[51] means to make sorrowful; to affect with sadness, to cause grief, to throw into sorrow; to grieve, or offend. We can cause the Holy Spirit to be grieved, saddened or sorrowful when we sin, have unforgiveness in our heart, cause disunity to the church, and speak against our brothers or sisters in Christ. Anything that offends Christ and His body offends and grieves the Holy Spirit.

Skandalon

"Dad, I don't feel strong. I know the Holy Spirit is helping me. I just try to lean on Him each day. But I have to tell you, sometimes I get really down and don't think I can press through one more day. I get so frustrated when I falter in my faith. God speaks to me, and I'm encouraged, but then something happens, and I'm struggling again. I often feel like a failure."

"Michael, that's why we are told to walk out our faith. It's a walk. All of us stumble from time to time. Even when we hear a clear word from God, we're still not immune to struggles, especially when the enemy makes the path look so impassable and the mountain so immoveable. But the important thing is that you keep putting one foot in front of the other, you keep getting back up when you fall, and you run to the One Who holds onto you and will never let you go. That's what's important."

Page 245

He is a lover of souls.

*Read **Romans 15:30** and fill in the blanks.*
Now I beg you, brethren, through the Lord Jesus Christ, and through the _____ of the _____, that you strive together with me in prayers to God for me.

He has a voice and speaks the truth of Jesus to the children of God.

*Look at **Acts 13:2** and fill in the blanks.*
As they ministered to the Lord and fasted, _____ Holy Spirit _____, "Now separate to Me Barnabas and Saul for the work to which I have called them."

Match the Scripture with the corresponding work of the Holy Spirit.

John 16:13	*He is our helper, teacher and brings to our remembrance the Word of Christ when we need it.*
Matthew 1:20	*He gives comfort to the body of Christ when we are weary, distressed, persecuted, or grieving.*
John 14:26	*He guides the believer according to what He hears the Father speaking.*
Acts 9:31	*He testifies of Christ.*
John 15:26	*The Holy Spirit was active in the birth and life of Jesus.*

Being filled with the Holy Spirit, Jesus was led into the wilderness by the Spirit. It was there that the devil tempted Him for forty days. He was anointed by the Holy Spirit to preach, heal the sick and brokenhearted, proclaim liberty to the captives, and open the eyes of the blind. It was by the Spirit of God that Jesus was able to offer Himself as the spotless sacrifice (*Hebrews 9:13-14*). The Spirit was present at the resurrection declaring Jesus to be the Son of God (*Romans 1:4*). If the Holy Spirit was so very present and active in the life of Christ, how much more should we desire Him to be active and present in our lives? Just as He anointed and empowered Jesus, He desires to anoint and empower every believer to do even greater works than He did.

He is God the Holy Spirit. Therefore, He has all of the attributes of God. He is omnipotent. He has unlimited authority and power.

*Read **Acts 10:38** and fill in the blanks.*
How God anointed _____ of Nazareth with the _____ _____ and with _____, who went about doing good and healing all who were oppressed by the devil, for God was with Him.

He is omnipresent. He can be in all places at once.

*Read **Psalms 139:7** and fill in the blanks.*
Where can I go from Your _____? Or where can I flee from Your _____?

The Holy Spirit is Omniscient or all knowing.

*Read **1 Corinthians 2:9-10** and fill in the blanks.*
But as it is written:
"Eye has not seen, nor ear heard, nor have entered into the heart of man the things _____ _____ has _____ for those who love Him."
But God has _____ _____ to us through His Spirit. For the Spirit searches all things, yes, the _____ _____ of God.

The Holy Spirit is eternal *(Hebrews 9:14)*.

As you can see, He is very much an active partner of the Godhead and He desires to be actively involved in the life of every believer. But you must acknowledge His presence in your life, and your need for Him to take control of every aspect of your life in Christ.

What role do you believe the Holy Spirit has played in your life and walk? Have you ever acknowledged the importance of His presence in your walk with God? _____
_____
_____
_____
_____
_____
_____

If you've never acknowledged the Holy Spirit, I'd ask you to say a prayer with me (*yes, out loud*). If you are a believer, He lives in you. But let's pray and give Him free reign to work in your heart and life.

Father God,

Today I want to acknowledge the role of the Holy Spirit in my life. I need Him to work in my life to change me and make me an effective and powerful witness. Holy Spirit, please come. Just as you hovered over the face of the waters in the Creation event, come hover over me. Change me. Mold me. Take over every aspect of my life. I want to know You more. Father, thank You that You hear my prayers and the desires of my heart. In Jesus name. Amen!

Day 2

And when He had said this, He breathed on them, and said to them, "Receive the Holy Spirit."
John 20:22

The Indwelling of the Holy Spirit

The Holy Spirit prepares the believer for our eternal role as the Bride of Christ. He has come to dwell in each of us to seal, sanctify, empower, and prepare us for our beloved Bridegroom. I don't know about you, but when the Lord saved me…He had to dig deep down into the pit to pull me out of the muck and mire of life. I knew that

> *But we all, with unveiled face, beholding as in a mirror the glory of the Lord, are being transformed into the same image from glory to glory, just as by the Spirit of the Lord.*
> *2 Corinthians 3:18*

I'd been saved and that I was a new creation in Christ (*2 Corinthians 5:17*). However, I still needed to change on the inside. He has done an amazing work in me and continues to work in my heart and life by transforming me from glory to glory. He has been and continues to be patient, gracious and loving in this transformation process.

It is only by the Holy Spirit that we come into a relationship with God *(John 6:44)*. When we were lost and living in the world, it was the Holy Spirit who convicted us of sin and drew us into a relationship with God through Jesus Christ.

Read John 16:8 and fill in the blank.
And when He has come, He will _____ the world of sin, and of righteousness, and of judgment.

The word *convict*[53] means to convince of error or sinfulness. We can better understand this word from the context of being used in a court of law. When a person is on trial, his attorney presents evidence of his innocence. The prosecuting attorney does everything in his power to convince the jury that the person is guilty of their crime and thus should be convicted and sentenced accordingly.

It is the Holy Spirit's job to convict the world of its sinfulness and the need to turn to God for salvation. Once we've decided to make Jesus our Savior, the Holy Spirit comes to take up permanent residence in our spirit. Jesus was very much acquainted with the schemes of the enemy and his hatred of the body of Christ. And, knowing that He would be ascending to heaven, it was His desire that we would not be left alone on this earth to fend for ourselves. So He prayed to the Father that He would give us a Helper. Someone just like Himself to guide us and empower us to walk out our Christian life on this earth.

*Read **John 14:16-17** and fill in the blanks.*
And I will pray the Father, and He will give you another _____, that
He may _____ with you forever— the _____ of
truth, whom the world cannot receive, because it neither sees Him nor knows Him; but you know Him,
for He _____ with you and will be _____ you.

> Let your conduct be without covetousness; be content with such things as you have. For He Himself has said, "I will never leave you nor forsake you."
> Hebrews 13:5

The word *Helper*[54] used in this passage is the Greek word *parakletos*. It originates from the word *para*, meaning *beside* and *kaleo*, meaning *to call*. As our Helper, He is the One who is called to be by our side. The word signifies an intercessor, comforter, helper, advocate, and counselor.

The Holy Spirit empowers us to become more and more like Christ. Because He is the Author of the Bible *(2 Peter 1:21)*, He enables us to understand when we read and study it and brings it to our remembrance when we need it.

The moment we become born-again, the Holy Spirit comes to make His permanent dwelling place within us. We have become indwelled by the Holy Spirit of the living God.

*Read **1 Corinthians 6:19** and fill in the blanks.*
Or do you not know that your _____ is the _____
of the Holy Spirit who is _____ you, whom you have from God, and you are not your
_____?

Once the Holy Spirit takes up residence, we become His temple. We are no longer our own. We are accountable to live our lives in such a way that we glorify God the Father. Therefore, we need to be sensitive to His voice and be obedient when He instructs us so that we do not bring dishonor to His temple. He'll lead us into a life that glorifies Jesus, but we must grow in our relationship with Him, listen, and obey as He speaks *(John 16:13-15)*.

I try to be very cognizant when I am watching a movie or television program, for example, so that I'm not subjecting the Holy Spirit to participate in an activity that would grieve Him.

Therefore, I need to choose what I watch carefully. I don't abstain from watching certain television shows or movies out of a legalistic mindset. I simply don't want to grieve the One who dwells within me. I'm certainly not perfect, but it's my goal to honor Him in everything I do and say. As I've grown in my relationship with Him, I've come to discover those things that grieve Him. I try to listen and obey when He whispers, "*Don't do that. Don't say that.*"

We see in the life of the disciples, that before Jesus ascended into heaven to sit at the right hand of the Father, He breathed on them and said, "*Receive the Holy Spirit.*" At this point, the Holy Spirit came to indwell in each one of them. It's important that you understand that this happened before the day of Pentecost, which we'll discuss in our next lesson.

Read **Ephesians 1:13-14** *and fill in the blanks.*
In Him you also trusted, after you heard the word of truth, the gospel of your salvation; in whom also, having believed, you were _____ with the _____ _____ of promise, who is the _____ of our inheritance until the redemption of the purchased possession, to the praise of His glory.

The Holy Spirit seals us for the day of redemption. When we ask Christ to come into our lives, we become sealed or marked as His very own. He, of course, takes this very seriously.

The word *sealed*[55] carries the meaning of being kept secure from Satan. It doesn't mean that the evil one can't touch us, but it's a mark signifying that we belong to Christ. And, Christ has the power to keep what belongs to Him.

Skandalon
"Father, I thank You for this wonderful promise from Your word. No matter what it looks like to me, I thank You that You continue to hold my wife in the palm of Your hand. I thank You that she cannot be separated from You. I bind Satan and all of his forces from trying to keep her bound in sin, and thank You that You will send out warring angels to fight for her freedom. I thank You that Your mercies are new every morning and ask You to extend mercy to her today. I pray for Your will to be done in her life. Holy Spirit, I ask You to woo her back to her first love. Heal her brokenness. In Jesus's name. Amen!"
Page179

The Holy Spirit is also the guarantee of our inheritance. The word *guarantee*[56] is a business term that speaks of earnest money or a down payment. It is the first installment that guarantees possession once the loan is paid in full.

I was saved as a young child. I would either attend church with my best friend or go to a little Assembly of God church directly behind my house. However, when I was in the eighth grade, my family moved to Europe. My parents didn't attend church, so we never searched out a church for me to attend overseas. I grew away from the Lord. As a young adult, I lived a very sinful life (*to say the least*). But I could often tangibly feel the presence of the Spirit wooing me back to the Lord. At one point in my life, His presence was so strong that one day, while I was driving my car, I felt Him pull on my sleeve (*that day, I was headed to do something I'm not proud of*). I turned to the passenger side of the car (*though no person was in the car*) and spoke out loud, "*I'm not ready yet.*" At that point, my life took such a downward spiral that it wasn't long before I surrendered my life back over to Him.

> *Let your conduct be without covetousness;*
> *be content with such things as you have.*
> *For He Himself has said,*
> *"I will never leave you nor forsake you."*
> Hebrews 13:5

The Holy Spirit abides with us forever. He will never leave you or forsake you. He'll never give up on you and is always willing to help you when you cry out to the Father.

He longs for a deep, abiding relationship with you. Acknowledge His abiding presence in your life, and you will experience immense spiritual growth (*John 15:1-8*).

Read **Romans 8:12-17** *and fill in the blanks.*
Therefore, brethren, we are debtors—not to the flesh, to live according to the flesh. For if you _____ according to the _____ you will _____; but if by the _____ you put to _____ the deeds of the body, you will live. For as many as are _____ by the _____ of _____, these are _____ of God. For you did not receive the spirit of bondage again to fear, but you received the Spirit of _____ by whom we cry out, "Abba, Father." The Spirit Himself _____ _____ with our spirit that we are _____ of God, and if children, then heirs—heirs of God and joint heirs with Christ, if indeed we suffer with Him, that we may also be glorified together.

The Holy Spirit leads us into a life of holiness and enables us, when we submit to Him, to resist the flesh and its desires. We must be sensitive to His leading so that we can avoid being ensnared by our enemy. It is imperative that we are quick to obey His leading, which often requires death to our fleshly desires. However, the result is a deepening of our relationship with Him.

He also bears witness to our spirit that we are children of God. It is by the Holy Spirit that we realize the implications of our born-again experience; the old has died, and a new life in Christ has begun.

I'm reminded of the infomercials we often see on television. You know, the one where they try to sell you something that promises to make your life easier. They make it appear to be the greatest deal on earth if you'll only call the number on your television screen. Then, just when you question the worth and validity of the product, they add, *"But wait…there's more!"*

There's so much more that the Holy Spirit wants to do in our lives if we'll only allow Him the ability. But wait…there's more! We'll go deeper in tomorrow's lesson.

Please ask the Holy Spirit to continue to open your understanding to the depths of all that He is and desires to be in your life. Ask Him to prepare your heart for our lesson tomorrow. Thank Him for His indwelling presence and the grace He so freely gives.

Day 3

On the last day, that great day of the feast, Jesus stood and cried out, saying, "If anyone thirsts, let him come to Me and drink. He who believes in Me, as the Scripture has said, out of his heart will flow rivers of living water." But this He spoke concerning the Spirit, whom those believing in Him would receive; for the Holy Spirit was not yet given, because Jesus was not yet glorified. John 7:37-39

MORE...THE INFILLING OF THE HOLY SPIRIT

> *"Behold, I send the Promise of My Father upon you; but tarry in the city of Jerusalem until you are endued with power from on high."*
> *Luke 24:49*

After Christ died and was resurrected, He knew His disciples would need someone to continue to strengthen, guide and comfort them. He was aware that they could not fulfill the great commission nor stand against the enemy's attacks alone. So He promised them His Holy Spirit. He instructed them to tarry in the city of Jerusalem until they were endued with power from on high.

Before these disciples could go out and conquer the world for Christ, they were to tarry. Doesn't that sound just like the Father? *"Go...but wait!"* God's plan usually makes no sense to the human mind *(Isaiah 55:8-9)*. The word *tarry*[57] means to sit down. Jesus was telling them not to do anything without the Holy Spirit. Just sit down and wait! I have learned through walking with the Lord that this same directive applies to and works for me. I can't do anything worthwhile without the power of the Holy Spirit operating in and through me. Therefore, until He gives me the orders, I just wait.

The word *endued,* which is used in *Luke 24:49*, means to clothe or put on clothing. It is the same word Paul uses in *Ephesians 6:11*, when we are told to put on the spiritual armor. We are to be clothed with the power of the Holy Spirit. I would even go so far as to say that without His power, we are spiritually naked!

Jesus knew that His disciples *(by the way, we are disciples too)* needed the power to fulfill the great commission. So He promised them the power of the Holy Spirit. Please make note that this was a promise given not only to the disciples but to you and me as well. The word *power*[58] is the Greek word *dunamis*. From this Greek word, we get our English word, *dynamite*. It speaks of energy, power, might, great force, and great ability. It is dynamic power to do or fulfill the commission of God. Without this power, we are working out of our own strength. This power is still available for the church today though many are not aware of it.

154

The Promise of the Father should take place at the time of salvation but because of doctrinal confusion, many do not go that step further to ask and receive the fullness of the Spirit.

We've discussed the fact that it wasn't until after being endued with the power of the Holy Spirit that Jesus was led into the wilderness to overcome the enemy's temptation *(Matthew 3:13-4:1)*. It wasn't until after the Holy Spirit descended upon Jesus, that we see the beginning of His ministry. If it were necessary for Jesus to be filled with the Holy Spirit, I would think it's necessary for the body of Christ to be filled with the Promise before attempting to do anything for the Lord.

Read Luke 4:16-19. Now look at verse 18 and 19 and fill in the blanks.
"The _____ of the Lord is upon Me, because He has _____
Me to _____ the gospel to the _____;
He has sent Me to _____ the brokenhearted, to proclaim
_____ to the captives and recovery of _____ to
the _____, To set at liberty those who are _____;
To proclaim the acceptable year of the Lord."

After being in the wilderness and tempted by Satan, Jesus returned to Galilee in the power *(dunamis)* of the Spirit. Shortly after that, He stood in a synagogue in Nazareth and read the above passage from the book of Isaiah. He then proclaimed that He was the fulfillment of that Scripture. He was now able to go forth in the power and anointing of the Holy Spirit to fulfill His destiny and purpose. He was filled with the Spirit so that He would be able to walk in the power of the Spirit.

Read Acts 1:1-8 and answer the following questions.
According to Acts 1:5, what was the Promise of the Father Jesus was speaking about?

_____

Jesus told the disciples that John baptized with water. What were the disciples to be baptized with?

_____

Looking at Acts 1:8, what were the disciples to receive when the Holy Spirit came upon them?

_____

Knowing that the disciples already had a firm belief in Jesus as the Messiah (*Savior*), we can see that the Promise they were to tarry for was something set apart from the salvation experience. Don't forget, Jesus had already breathed on them and told them to receive the Holy Spirit before He ascended into heaven. The Promise was the Holy Spirit, the third person of the Holy Trinity. The Promise is still available for every believer in Jesus today. All you have to do is ask.

As we studied yesterday, when we are born-again, or come into a relationship with the Father through confession of our belief in Jesus as Savior and Lord, we are indwelt and sealed by the Holy Spirit. He comes to make His home in us and helps us to become new creations in Christ. He is the guarantee of our eternal life with Christ. However, we can make Jesus the Savior of our life without giving Him complete Lordship or surrendering our will over to Him. In the same manner, we can have the Holy Spirit indwell us without experiencing the fullness or baptism of the Holy Spirit.

Read Acts 1:13-14 and 2:1-4 and answer the following questions.
Who was gathered together on the day of Pentecost? _____
_____

What were the manifestations of the Holy Spirit seen and experienced by those present?
_____
_____

Notice that the Holy Spirit came in great power. There was a sound, like that of a rushing mighty wind. There was what appeared to be divided tongues that looked like fire resting upon each disciple. And, there was a distinct utterance given to each disciple who experienced this Baptism.

Read Matthew 3:11 and fill in the blanks. These were words spoken by John the Baptist.
I indeed baptize you with water unto repentance, but He who is coming after me is mightier than I, whose sandals I am not worthy to carry. He will _____ *you with the*
_____ _____ *and* _____.

The Bible tells us that God never changes *(Malachi 3:6)*. When one experiences the infilling or Baptism of the Holy Spirit, it is generally experienced with great power and evidenced by speaking in tongues *(we will discuss speaking in tongues in our next lesson)*.

In the Word, every time there is mention of the baptism of the Holy Spirit, there was always a release of power for the express purpose of bearing witness of and for Christ. There was a definite transformation in the life of the Apostles after receiving the baptism of the

Holy Spirit. Peter became a bold witness for Christ whereas before this baptism of fire he had denied Christ out of fear. They were all empowered to be witnesses, endure unimaginable persecution, perform great signs and wonders, and walk out their faith with great boldness.

Though he had a divine encounter with the Lord, the Apostle Paul had to be filled with the Holy Spirit before he could be sent out to do great and mighty works for God *(Acts 9:10-17)*. It was because of the infilling of the Holy Spirit that he was able to do great works in the name of Jesus, survive great persecution and write much of the New Testament.

Peter was sent to minister to Cornelius, a devout, God-fearing man, and those gathered in his home. Peter explained the plan of salvation through Christ to this Gentile man and those present with him. The result was that the whole household was born-again and then filled with the Holy Spirit.

Read Acts 10:44-46 and answer the following question.
What was the visible evidence that these believers had received the Holy Spirit?

_____

Read Acts 19:1-6 and answer the following questions.
According to **verse 2**, *Paul was speaking to a group of disciples. Who was it that these disciples had never heard of?* _____

According to **verse 3**, *who's baptism had they been baptized into?*_____

_____

When Paul learned that they'd been baptized into John's baptism, he then baptized them in the name of _____ *(see* **verse 5***).*

What took place when Paul laid hands on them (see **verse 6***)?* _____

_____

*What was the visible evidence that the Holy Spirit had come upon them?*_____

_____

When Paul met these disciples, they believed in the Messiah to come but they had not so much as heard of the Holy Spirit. He then led them into a fuller understanding of a relationship with Christ. He baptized them in water. Then, he laid hands on them so that they could receive the promise of the Holy Spirit.

*For further study you can read **Acts 8:14-25**.*
*Read **Ephesians 5:18** and fill in the blank.*
And do not be drunk with wine, in which is dissipation; but be _____ with the Spirit,

The Greek verb tense for the words *be filled*[59] suggests a continual filling. Though we experience the baptism of the Holy Spirit once, we are to be continually filled.

Jesus equated the Holy Spirit to living water. Therefore, I'm going to use the same analogy. Picture a glass filled to the top with water. However, as you go through your day taking sips of the water, the water level in the glass decreases. Before long, your glass is in need of a refill if you want to remain hydrated.

Our spiritual glass becomes empty primarily when we sin. However, life has a way of draining the spiritual power out of us. Have you ever experienced a loss of spiritual vitality when you were going through sickness, an immense trial, or the loss of a loved one?

I love that Paul used the analogy of being drunk with wine as opposed to being filled with the Spirit. Those of you who were heavy drinkers (*before Christ*) know that if you were to drink four or five glasses of wine, you would get drunk. You could go home and sleep it off, and you'd no longer be filled with alcohol. Right? However, you could go out the next night and get drunk all over again by filling yourself back up with wine or your drink of choice.

We see several instances where the Holy Spirit makes us aware that the disciples were continually filled. We know this because they were filled on the day of Pentecost. Yet, the Holy Spirit brings out the fact that they were filled again in *Acts 4:23-31*.

We stay in a continual state of being filled by doing several things. Prayer (*specifically prayer in the Holy Spirit which we will talk about in our next lesson*), reading and listening to the Word, fellowship with the Holy Spirit (by *talking to Him and acknowledging His presence*), confession and repentance of sin, obedience, and walking in unity with the body of Christ.

If you've never experienced the baptism of the Holy Spirit, I want to invite you to say a bold prayer today. That's all you have to do to receive the Promise of the Father. But you must pray in faith believing that the Father will give you what He promised *(Matthew 7:9-11)*.

Father God, in the name of Jesus, I ask You to fill me with Your Promised Holy Spirit. I desire that rivers of living water would flow from out of my inner man. I give myself to You and ask You to rule and reign in my life. I surrender all to You. Come and fill me now, Holy Spirit. Help me to live the Spirit-led life. Thank You for this precious gift Father.

158

Day 4

And these signs will follow those who believe: In My name they will cast out demons; they will speak with new tongues; Mark 16:17

THEY WILL SPEAK WITH NEW TONGUES

Before we begin our lesson today, I would ask you to say a prayer. I recognize that to many of you, today's lesson will be a fresh new word. To others, it will be controversial and go against what you've been taught to be true, and to some, it may seem a bit scary. I believe Satan has stirred such great controversy associated with speaking in tongues because of the power that is released in the lives of those who practice it. Therefore, I would ask you to please pray for your eyes to be open, your ears to hear, and for the truth to be made known in your heart as we work through this lesson.

Father God, open my eyes and ears to your truth. I pray for discernment as I work through this lesson. I thank You that You make Your will known to me as I study and read Your Word. Help me to set aside man's wisdom and open my heart and spirit to the wisdom that comes from You. In Jesus name. Amen!

*Read **Ephesians 6:18** and fill in the blanks.*
Praying always with _____ prayer and supplication in the _____, being watchful to this end with all perseverance and supplication for all the saints—

When Paul exhorts the Ephesian church to pray with *all* prayer and supplication…would we not be able to assume that prayer goes deeper than simply reciting a lengthy list of our requests to God? When we are in the midst of the battle, we need to know exactly what to do to be victorious over our enemy. We need divine guidance and Spirit-led directives and strategies. We can't afford to be second-guessing and hoping that whatever we are doing will be effective.

*Read **Acts 2:1-4**. Looking at **verse 4**, please fill in the blanks.*
And they were all _____ with the Holy Spirit and began to speak with other _____, as the Spirit gave them utterance.

On the day of Pentecost, the believers (*disciples*) were gathered together praying when the Holy Spirit fell like a rushing mighty wind and filled each one of them. As evidence of this infilling, they began to speak with other tongues as the Holy Spirit gave them utterance (*spoke through them*). In every instance, tongues were an outward manifestation when the disciples received the baptism of the Holy Spirit. The word *tongues*[60] is the Greek word *glossa* and simply means the language or dialect used by a particular people distinct from that of other nations. Some believe that this is what Paul was referring to when speaking of the '*tongues of angels*' *(1 Corinthians 13:1)*. It is a heavenly prayer language given to the body of Christ and a result of the Holy Spirit baptism.

There are some who ask the Holy Spirit to fill or baptize them and, either because of wrong doctrine, fear and doubt, or lack of knowledge; they do not immediately speak in tongues. This was the case with me. As a child, I prayed for the baptism. But it wasn't until I was an adult that I surrendered my life to Christ and received my prayer language. It happened supernaturally. I was overcome with emotion during a worship song at church. I stood to sing and out of my mouth came words that I did not recognize or understand. I knew that this was my heavenly prayer language.

Jesus made it clear that tongues were to be a sign that follows or marks the believer in Christ.

We receive this baptism experience just like we receive anything else from God; by faith. It is a gift that is promised to every believer. The Father longs for us to have it. All we must do is believe that it is ours for the taking, ask and receive.

Read Luke 11:11-13 and fill in the blanks.
If a son asks for bread from any father among you, will he give him a stone? Or if he asks for a fish, will he give him a serpent instead of a fish? Or if he asks for an egg, will he offer him a scorpion? If you then, being evil, know how to give good gifts to your children, how much more will your heavenly Father give the _____ _____ to those who _____ Him!"

Speaking in tongues does not make one more spiritual. However, it does allow a person to go deeper in prayer than their human limitations allow. The Word tells us that when we pray in tongues, we are allowing the Holy Spirit to pray through us with words and utterances that we can't understand with our human mind. Now, please understand, this is not in any way like new age meditation. The person praying in tongues is fully aware of their thoughts, their body, and their emotions. However, we must be surrendered in mind, body, and spirit to Christ when we pray in the spirit. In other words, the Holy Spirit will not open my mouth and cause words to come forth. I must open my mouth to speak just as I must consciously decide to pray in the spirit instead of in my natural language.

> Likewise the Spirit also helps in our weaknesses. For we do not know what we should pray for as we ought, but the Spirit Himself makes intercession for us with groanings which cannot be uttered. Now He who searches the hearts knows what the mind of the Spirit is, because He makes intercession for the saints according to the will of God.
> Romans 8:26-27

There are times in my life when I am so burdened regarding a situation that I don't know what or how to pray. It is at these times that I pray in the spirit, allowing the Holy Spirit to pray through me. He intercedes for me. I don't always know the will of the Father in every situation. But the Holy Spirit does and will always pray the perfect will of God. He knows what is going on in the spirit realm and can see what we cannot see which makes our prayer life that much more effective. This heavenly prayer language is an immensely important spiritual weapon against the enemy.

Read 1 Corinthians 14:2-5. The subject of tongues was so important that Paul dedicated an entire chapter to it. In this passage of Scripture, he was trying to bring order to the New Testament church. He was making a distinction between the importance of prophecy in one's native language as opposed to speaking in tongues within the congregational setting.

In verse 2, Paul states that when one speaks in a tongue, he does not speak to _____ but to _____.

In verse 3, we see the purpose of prophecy. Fill in the blanks.
But he who prophesies speaks _____ and _____ _____ and _____ to men.

Verse 4 makes a clear distinction regarding the difference between tongues and prophesying.
He who speaks in a tongue edifies _____.
He who prophesies edifies _____.

The word *edifies*[61] means to build a house or to restore by building. When we pray in the spirit, we are building our spiritual house. We are restoring what has been broken down by the world, negative circumstances, and the attacks of the enemy.

There is a difference between using the gift of tongues in a congregational setting and in one's private prayer time. *Read 1 Corinthians 14:6-19.* In the congregational setting, if one speaks in tongues (*verse 13*), he should pray that he may interpret the message so that the body is edified or encouraged. This is the gift of tongues and interpretation of tongues referred to in *1 Corinthians 12:10*.

Look at 1 Corinthians 14:15. What was Paul's conclusion?
I will _____ with the _____, and I will also _____ with the _____.

Notice in *verse 18*, Paul states that He uses his spiritual prayer language regularly. However, (*verse 19*) in the church, he considered it necessary to speak in his native language (*with my understanding*) so that others may be taught and edified.

Praying in tongues gives you access to the revelatory gifts mentioned in *1 Corinthians 12:8-10.*

Read Jude 1:20-21 and fill in the blanks.
But you, beloved, _____ _____ up on your most holy faith, _____ in the _____ _____, keep yourselves in the love of God, looking for the mercy of our Lord Jesus Christ unto eternal life.

Skandalon

He continued to pray the Word of God over Zoe with great authority, often going back and forth between praying in English and praying in his heavenly prayer language, allowing the Holy Spirit to pray through him with words and utterances he couldn't understand with his natural mind. He felt invigorated. He could sense the tremendous spiritual battle being waged in the heavenlies for his wife's soul.

Page 260

When we pray in the Holy Spirit or pray in tongues, we build up our faith for a given situation. We receive spiritual strength and edification as we pray in the spirit.

Because of doctrinal differences in the body of Christ, this has become an issue that causes separation. Isn't it just like Satan to use one of the most powerful gifts as a means of bringing division and rendering much of the church without the power needed to defeat him?

Many believe that tongues ceased with the Apostles. When I hear this, I think back to the days after the resurrection of Christ. The Jewish leaders did everything within their power to keep the disciples quiet and from speaking the name of Jesus. A wise Pharisee named Gamaliel spoke to the Jewish leaders who wanted to kill the Apostles. Look at what he said in *Acts 5:38-39*.

> *And now I say to you, keep away from these men and let them alone; for if this plan or this work is of men, it will come to nothing; but if it is of God, you cannot overthrow it—lest you even be found to fight against God."*

I have noticed that denominations that have taught against the baptism of the Holy Spirit for decades are beginning to accept it as being a gift from the Lord. I read an article recently that the Southern Baptist Convention will now admit missionary candidates who practice speaking in *tongues*.[62]

Yesterday, we said a prayer asking the Holy Spirit to fill us. Some may have received their heavenly prayer language upon receiving the baptism of the Holy Spirit. If not, there may be a hindrance to you receiving this gift.

You must first repent of doubt and unbelief regarding speaking in tongues. I assure you that Satan has played a huge part in keeping the body of Christ from receiving the Holy Spirit in fullness. He doesn't want you praying in tongues because he can't understand it.

You also need to be convinced of your belief that this is a gift from God that He desires to bestow on you, His child. He longs to give you good gifts. However, it is you that must take the gift, open it, and claim it as your own.

If you've been taught that tongues are not for today or that they are of the devil (*clever strategy of his, wouldn't you say*), I would encourage you to immerse yourself in the Scriptures we have studied. Pray as you read them and ask God to unveil any lies so that you might see clearly and receive His truth.

Not everyone receives their prayer language the same. My prayer language sounds completely different from my husbands. When I first received my prayer language, I had maybe three words that I repeated over and over again. I felt foolish. At first, I became discouraged thinking I must be making them up. However, as I continued faithfully to pray in the spirit, my prayer language grew.

When a baby learns to talk, they usually start out with one or two words. But once they understand the power of their words (*they learn that they get what they want as they learn to communicate through words*), their vocabulary grows.

If you desire this powerful prayer language, please repeat the following prayer:

Father,

I know it is Your desire to give Your children good gifts. Therefore, I come to You and ask You to fill me with Your Promised Holy Spirit with the evidence of speaking in tongues. I need Your power flowing through me. Forgive me for any doubt or unbelief that I've had regarding this baptism of fire. Open up my understanding to receive. Lord, show me if there are any hindrances to me receiving this gift. I desire all that you have for me. Fill me and empower me to be Your disciple. Thank You for boldness. Holy Spirit come! In Jesus name, Amen!

Once you've said this prayer, open your mouth. However, don't speak in English (*or whatever your native language is*). You'll hear or sense sounds that want to come forth. They won't make sense to you, and you'll think you are making them up. Go ahead, in faith, speak them out.

Day 5

"Most assuredly, I say to you, he who believes in Me, the works that I do he will do also; and greater works than these he will do, because I go to My Father." John 14:12

THE POWER IN YOU!

*Read **Acts 1:8a** and fill in the blanks.*
But you shall receive _____ when the Holy Spirit has come upon you;
and you shall be _____ to Me in Jerusalem, and in all Judea
and Samaria, and to the end of the earth."

The very same power that was *in* Christ is available to the believer who has been empowered by the Holy Spirit. The power to be a witness, to walk in victory, to heal the sick, to deliver the demon-possessed, to raise the dead, and to do even greater works than Christ did. This power is the distinct purpose for the outpouring of the Holy Spirit that we read about in the Book of Acts. He came to empower the church so that we might be able to do the ministry of the kingdom.

As we discussed in an earlier lesson, Christ told the disciples to tarry for this dynamic power. Before they went out to do anything for the kingdom of God, they were to wait until they were endued with power from the Holy Spirit.

We receive power to become witnesses for Christ. I know many would say that they are already a witness for Christ. Their proof would be in the number of people they've brought to a saving faith in the Lord by sharing the Gospel message with them. I would never downplay anyone's ability to share their faith with others. It certainly takes courage. However, the dunamis power of the Holy Spirit will enable the believer to go so much further than simply sharing their faith with a lost person.

The witness of Christ is one who is empowered by the Spirit, doing the works of Christ; healing the sick, opening blind eyes and deaf ears, casting out demons, and operating in the gifts of the Holy Spirit. Christ pointed the lost to the Father by a demonstration of the Holy Spirit's power. His witness was more than mere words. It was demonstrated or backed-up by mighty, miraculous works. We are to do more than just tell people about Jesus. We are to demonstrate the same power that He walked in.

*Read **Acts 4:33** and fill in the blanks.*

And with great _____ *the apostles gave* _____
to the resurrection of the Lord Jesus. And great grace was upon them all.

*Read **Acts 5:12-16** and answer the following questions.*
In the passage, through whose hands were signs and wonders being performed? _____
_____

What were the results of these signs and wonders being performed? _____
_____
_____
_____
_____

I do hope that you noticed the fact that believers were added to the Lord. The lost are drawn by signs and wonders. When cancer is instantly and miraculously healed, blind eyes are opened and deaf ears hear for the first time...non-believers take notice of the power that they cannot refute.

Now, you might be quick to say, "*It was the Apostles doing the signs and wonders. I'm not an Apostle, and so I don't think I can do the same things they did.*"

*Read **Acts 6:1-10** and answer the following questions.*

In this passage, the Apostles were presented with a problem. Due to the rapid growth of the early church, the need arose for there to be men to oversee and delegate the daily distribution of goods within the body of believers.

*According to **verse 3**, what were the qualifications of the men chosen for this responsibility?*
_____
_____

*Look at **verse 5**. Steven was a man full of faith and the* _____?

*According to **verse 7**, what was the result of this new church organization by men filled with the Spirit of God?* _____
_____
_____

*Look at **verse 8** and fill in the blanks.*
And Stephen, full of _____ and _____, did great
_____ and _____ among the people.

Stephen was a disciple who'd surrendered his life to the Lord. He was filled with the Holy Spirit's power and moved in the demonstration of that power. We are meant to do the same.

*Read **Acts 9:10-19** and answer the following questions.*
*According to **verse 10**, Ananias was a _____ of the Lord.*

God sent him to a street called Straight on a mission to restore sight to Saul of Tarsus.

*What mighty work did Ananias do in **verse 17**? _____*
_____
_____
_____
_____

What was the result of Ananias laying hands on Saul? _____
_____
_____

Ananias was a disciple just like you and me. He was obviously filled with the Holy Spirit. He laid hands on Saul so that he could be filled with the Holy Spirit and receive the restoration of his sight.

As a result of being endued with power by the Holy Spirit, there was a great boldness that came upon the disciples.

*Read **Acts 4:31** and fill in the blank.*
And when they had prayed, the place where they were assembled together was
_____; and they were all _____ with the Holy Spirit,
and they spoke the word of God with _____.

This boldness was not mere human boldness but a result of being filled with the Holy Spirit. The word *boldness*[63] means outspokenness, unreserved utterance, and freedom of speech with frankness. It is the opposite of cowardice, timidity or fear. It is a divine enablement that comes to ordinary and unprofessional people exhibiting spiritual power and authority.

We see in the lives of the disciples a tremendous change after being filled with the Holy Spirit. Simon, the fisherman, becomes Peter, the Rock. He'd once retreated in fear when questioned as to whether or not he knew Jesus. Once filled with the Spirit, he is a bold witness performing signs and wonders.

> But the fruit of the Spirit is love, joy, peace, longsuffering, kindness, goodness, faithfulness, gentleness, self-control. Against such there is no law. And those who are Christ's have crucified the flesh with its passions and desires. If we live in the Spirit, let us also walk in the Spirit.
>
> Galatians 5:22-25

It was by the same power of the Holy Spirit that the Apostles, as well as many believers in the early Church, were able to lay down their lives for the sake of Christ.

The power of the Holy Spirit enables the believer to become more and more like Christ daily.

*Read **Galatians 5:16** and fill in the blanks.*
I say then: Walk in the _____, and you shall not fulfill the _____ of the flesh.

The more we are submitted to and led by the Spirit and allow His power to be manifested in our lives, the more we will manifest the fruit of the Spirit.

We are changed from glory to glory by the power of the Holy Spirit. Those of us who've been transformed by this power can give a hearty amen to the fact that the transformation could not have happened without the working of the Spirit in our lives.

Skandalon
Carol sat on her couch with her Bible opened on her lap. Her husband, a security guard working the night shift, had left several hours earlier, and her daughter had already been tucked snugly into bed. She'd felt a strong stirring in her spirit while having her quiet time with the Lord, to pray for Zoe. She'd prayed in the Spirit for quite some time when God quickened a Scripture to her. It was a familiar Scripture, but she wasn't sure exactly where it was located in the Bible. After searching through the concordance in the back of her Bible, she found the passage and obediently wrote it down on a piece of stationery as she felt God had instructed her to do. She had no doubt in her mind that God would, at some point in time, make a way for her to share the Scripture with Zoe.
Page 257-258

When I met my husband, I was a total control freak. He, on the other hand, was very passive. However, due to two prior failed marriages, he knew he wanted to be the spiritual leader of our home. I can tell you that it took all the power the Holy Spirit could muster in me to transform this stubborn little Cajun girl to desire to submit myself to the leadership of my husband in our home. If His power can work in me, it can work in you too.

Let's close out this week's lesson with a prayer that Paul prayed over the Colossian believers. I encourage you to pray it over yourself.

> *For this reason we also, since the day we heard it, do not cease to pray for you,*
> *and to ask that you may be filled with the knowledge of His will in all wisdom*
> *and spiritual understanding; that you may walk worthy of the Lord, fully pleasing Him,*
> *being fruitful in every good work and increasing in the knowledge of God;*
> *strengthened with all might, according to His glorious power, for all patience*
> *and longsuffering with joy;*
> *Colossians 1:9-11*

7

Week Seven

Skandalon reading assignment: Chapters 25-28

Day 1

And now abide faith, hope, love, these three; but the greatest of these is love. 1 Corinthians 13:13

THE GREATEST OF THESE…

Several years ago, the Lord asked me to study love for one year. It changed my life. I'm still studying on love. I believe that if the body of Christ would simply concentrate and immerse ourselves in the study of love and allow it to dwell in us richly, we could all be a powerful witness that would draw the lost to Christ.

To understand what Biblical love is, we must first understand what it is not. We cannot confuse God's love with the love that the world has to offer.

Love[64], according to Webster's Online Dictionary, is defined as follows:

Strong affection for another arising out of kinship or personal ties as in the love of a mother for her child; attraction based on sexual desire, affection and tenderness felt by lovers; affection based on admiration, benevolence, or common interests.

The love that the world offers is based on the lies of the enemy and is rooted in sin. It is a conditional love based on a feeling of affection or attraction that can come and go as quickly as a summer rainstorm in Texas (*fellow Texans will get this analogy*). Self is at the center of this type of love. Worldly love seeks after others to fill the empty place in one's heart; a place that only God's love is meant to fill.

Television and cinema have convinced us that love is based on physical attraction as well as admired personality traits. The problem with this type of love is that people can change

171

in appearance as well as personality. They don't always meet our needs or conditions and often cause us disappointment and pain. When someone fails to meet our needs, we divorce them, separate ourselves from the relationship and discard them as if they never meant anything to us at all.

Satan would have us to believe the emptiness we often experience in our heart can be met by the love of another human being. However, the deception in this is that it puts pressure on another human being to do what only God was meant to do. Only God can truly meet all of our needs. He may choose to use a human to do so, but when we place the burden on another person to meet our needs, we set them as well as ourselves up for failure.

We have a misconception of what true God-like love is because we are so flippant with the use of the word *love*. We love our dog, we love our car, we love the latest television show, we love hamburgers, we love our job, and the list of things we love goes on and on.

We have depreciated or watered down the meaning of the word love because in the English language that one word can have so many different meanings. It can be used to describe our affection for those things mentioned above as well as how we feel about our children, spouse or best friend.

*I know that we could all probably recite **1 Corinthians 13:1–8**. However, I respectfully ask you to look it up and fill in the blanks.*

Though I speak with the tongues of men and of angels, but have not _____, I have become _____ _____ or a clanging cymbal. And though I have the gift of _____, and understand all mysteries and all knowledge, and though I have all _____, so that I could remove _____, but have not love, I am nothing. And though I bestow all my goods to feed the _____, and though I _____ _____ _____ to be burned, but have not love, it profits me nothing.
Love _____ _____ and is kind; love does not _____; love does not _____ _____, is not _____ _____; does not behave _____, does not seek its _____, is not _____, thinks no _____; does not rejoice in _____, but rejoices in the truth; bears all things, believes all things, hopes all things, _____ all things.
Love never _____. But whether there are prophecies, they will fail; whether there are tongues, they will cease; whether there is knowledge, it will vanish away.

By our misunderstanding of the God-kind of love, we fail to receive completely all of the love and mercy God has for us. It is difficult, if not impossible, to walk in love toward others if you don't first have a complete comprehension of the unlimited, unconditional love God has for you.

The God-kind of love is the total opposite of worldly love. God demonstrated His love to us by giving the life of His only Son for our salvation.

God places no conditions on His love for us. God loved us when we were at our worst. He sent His Son to die for us when we least deserved it. His example of love for us is to be the love that we strive to attain to in this life.

We will look at three words, which translate as the English word *love* in the Bible, yet has such different meanings in the Greek language which is the language of the New Testament. These three words are *agape, phileo,* and *eros*. When we understand their meanings, it enables us to understand how God expects us to demonstrate our love to others.

Agape love is a self-giving love that does not ask anything in return and does not consider as to whether the one being loved is worthy or not. It gives out of itself and expects nothing in return. It is this God-kind of love or unconditional love that God has for the world, which He demonstrated by giving the life of His only Son for the salvation of the world.

Agape love always seeks the highest good of the other person, even when the other person does not respond in love or seemingly deserve to be loved. It will sacrifice itself for the benefit of the other person. Agape love will love even when it might require personal pain and surrender in the giving of itself (*and it most often does*). Most often, we must choose to agape others. It is a love of the will rather than love based on emotions.

Marriages break up because couples are not walking in this God-kind of love. Churches split because the Body is not walking in agape love. Friendships end due to a lack of agape love flowing from one person to another.

God did not wait for us to change before He loved us. When walking in agape love, there is no requirement placed upon the other person or circumstances to change before we choose to extend love. This kind of love will motivate us to walk in faith, believing God to change the person and circumstances because we are walking in love as an act of obedience to God's commandment to love.

I once heard a statement that has stuck with me through all of my years of marriage.

Love is an unconditional commitment to an imperfect individual to meet the needs of that person in such a way that may require personal sacrifice.
*We see this God-kind of love best expressed in Jesus Christ's statement in **John 15:13**. Please look up the Scripture and fill in the blanks.*

"Greater _____ has no one than this than to _____ _____ one's life for his friends."

Jesus, as our example, perfectly demonstrated the agape kind of love by humbling Himself to come to earth and live as a man and surrender His life to die on the cross as a sacrifice for our sins.

It is this kind of love that God desires each of us to exemplify in our lives; a love of surrender in obedience to Christ. We love others because Christ first loved us.

*Read **1 John 3:16** and fill in the blank.*
By this we know_____, because He laid down His life for us. And we also ought to _____ _____ our _____ for the brethren.

Another Greek word used in the New Testament for love is *phileo*. Phileo describes a tender, affectionate love; and is a fondness or friendship on a human level. It is based on the attraction toward another individual. It is also known as a brotherly type of love. It is a love given because we cherish qualities in the other person that are pleasing to us. It's the greatest form of love that we see operating in those who live in the world without a personal relationship with Christ.

Eros is another word for love used in the New Testament. From eros, we get the word erotic. It is a physical love and has to do with a sensual attraction to another individual. It is a love that is based on receiving rather than giving. It is a selfish love and will sacrifice another to please self.

When motivated by eros love, we are more likely to allow our sexual appetites to lead us into sinful relationships. This type of love does not consider the Biblical view that sex outside of the marriage covenant is sinful because it seeks to please self rather than God or the other person.

Satan has perverted love to be more of a mixture of *phileo* love and *eros* love; a love that can easily be turned on or off. He has tricked the world into believing that it's *all about me* and *how I feel*. Many of us have believed the lie that we can fall into and out of love just as quickly as we can change our clothes. You can't fall out of agape love!

In the story of *Skandalon*, Satan attempted using a mixture of phileo and eros love to trap Michael into a relationship that was not God-ordained. Because Michael was tired and weary of waiting for God's best, he was tempted by Satan's counterfeit. When we enter into these types of relationships, we end up disillusioned and disappointed; forfeiting God's best for what can only temporarily satisfy.

The love Satan presents to the world is a conditional love that is based on whether or not our needs are met and our desires are fulfilled. It is the direct opposite of agape love. The greatest danger of operating in this type of love is that we can then be deceived into believing that this is how God, in turn, loves us. Nothing could be further from the truth.

Read John: 21:15-19.

Skandalon
"Just call me Michael." He blushed. She smiled.
"Okay, Michael. Thanks again. I'm so excited."
He flashed a schoolboy grin at her. "I'm excited too.
We can always use the help, and I think you'll be a great addition."
She turned and walked away, leaving him drooling on his desk. What in the world just happened?
He knew he'd felt attracted to her although he was committed to praying and waiting for Zoe.
He excused his behavior to being caught off guard by her beauty. He tried to get back to his studies,
but his thoughts kept returning to Sophie.
Page 314

In this story, Jesus asks Peter in *verse 15* if he loves (*agape*) Him, to which Peter replies, "Yes, Lord; You know that I love (*phileo*) You." We see this repeated in *verse 16*. However, in *verse 17*, Jesus asked Peter, "Simon, son of Jonah, do you love (*phileo*) me?"

This story has many applications regarding the life of Peter as well as the life of the believers. However, I believe that the Lord was showing Peter the level of love that he was walking in. Many of us are still only able to walk in phileo love because we do not understand the love (*agape*) that God has for us. My prayer is that by the end of this week's lessons, you'll not only have a revelation of the love Christ has for you but that your love will go deeper than a phileo love toward others.

I'd like to close out today's lesson by asking you to personalize the passage below by placing your name in every blank. Make this a personal prayer throughout the week. Let's make a decision to love others with agape love.

_____ *suffers long and is kind;* _____ *does not envy;*

175

_____ *does not parade (herself/himself),* _____ *is not puffed up;*
_____ *does not behave rudely,* _____ *does not seek*
(his/her) own, _____ *is not provoked, thinks no evil;* _____
does not rejoice in iniquity, but rejoices in the truth; _____ *bears all things,*
believes all things, hopes all things, endures all things.

Day 2

For God so loved the world that He gave His only begotten Son, that whoever believes in Him should not perish but have everlasting life. John 3:16

YOU ARE LOVED...

I'd like to preface this lesson by acknowledging that there are many who have a firm grasp of how deeply the Father loves you. However, there are many who struggle to grasp this concept, so please let this lesson be a refresher course for you. Also please pray for those who've yet to receive this revelation. Pray that they will finally come to know the truth… that they are radically loved by the Father.

As I stated before, it is impossible to walk in agape love or the God-kind of love toward others without first understanding how deeply we are loved by God. For many years in my walk with God, I lacked the revelation of how much I was loved and cherished by my heavenly Father. Therefore, I found it difficult to love others unconditionally.

I was raised in a home where love was conditional. I felt approval from my parents when I was doing what pleased them, and their wrath and displeasure when I was disobedient or failed to do what they wanted me to do. The God-kind of love was rarely demonstrated to my siblings or to me. I do not say this to condemn my parents because I believe this kind of worldly love was modeled to them by their parents. They were simply acting out of what they knew to do. However, when I came into a personal relationship with Christ, I felt that He could only love me when I was good. When I messed up or fell short of what I believed to be His expectations of me, I felt that I was unloved and unworthy of His approval or blessings. I almost always felt like I was a failure and a disappointment to Him.

Today I know that nothing could be farther from the truth! If you get nothing else out of this entire study, please receive the truth of this lesson: *You are loved by the Father*!

Read Jeremiah 31:3 and fill in the blanks.
"Yes, I have loved _____ *with an* _____ *love; Therefore with loving kindness I have drawn* _____.

1 John 4:8 tells us, *"He who does not love does not know God, for God is love"*. God is love and He can't help but love you because it is Who He is. It is His very nature and character to love you. God would have to stop being, in order to stop loving!

When we come to God, He does not expect us to clean ourselves up so that He can love us. At our very best, the Word tells us that our righteousness is as filthy rags. When we sin and fail Him, He still loves us just as much as the day we first met Him.

> *But we are all like an unclean thing, and all our righteousnesses are like filthy rags…*
>
> *Isaiah 64:6*

God loved you even when you were lost in the world, living a life of sin in disobedience to His Word.

*Read **Romans 5:8** and fill in the blanks.*
How did God demonstrate His love toward us? _____
_____
_____

Because of His great love for us, God sent His only Son to die a gruesome death on the cross. He chose us when we were still sinners. He loved us at our worst! Why would we think that He would love us less when we've surrendered our lives to Him, simply because we fall short or miss the mark? Please accept this truth deep down into the fabric of your being…there is nothing that you can do to make God love you more than He already does at this very moment. Nor is there anything that you could do to make Him love you less.

If we do not have this truth deeply ingrained in our soul, it is easy for Satan to convince us that the Father does not love us and, therefore, we should give up on our faith walk. He'll use our doubt as a means to lie to us and tell us that we cannot expect to receive anything good from God because we are unloved. Satan will tell you that man, who is fallible, can't possibly love you if an infallible God can fall in and out of love with you based on your performance.

God is relentless in His love for you. We are told that nothing can separate us from His love.

*Read **Romans 8:35, 37–39** and fill in the blanks.*
_____ shall _____ us from the _____ of Christ?
Shall tribulation, or distress, or persecution, or famine, or nakedness, or peril, or sword?
Yet in all these things we are more than conquerors through Him who _____
us. For I am persuaded that neither _____ nor _____, nor angels
not principalities nor powers, nor things present nor things to come, nor height nor depth, nor any
other created thing, shall be able to _____ us from the _____
of God which is in Christ Jesus our Lord.

Nothing can separate you from His love. Nothing! Does He desire your obedience to His Word? Absolutely! Does He love you less when you fail to be obedient to His Word? Absolutely not!

Even when I was promiscuous, doing drugs and living my life my way in order to satisfy myself; God reached out and saved me because He loved me.

The unconditional love that He has for us is demonstrated in the story of the prodigal son found in *Luke 15*. Most of us know this story well. *Please read Luke 15:11-24.*

Notice that the father in this story saw his son returning even from a great distance. Picture this father going outside several times every day to scan the horizon, hoping for a glimpse of his son returning home to him and his family. He obviously had a great longing for his son to return home even though he knew his son had sinned against God as well as against him. When his son finally returns to his senses and journeys home, the father welcomes him with unconditional (*agape*) love and compassion. In *verse 23*, it says that he told his servants to bring the fatted calf to kill and eat in celebration. I believe the father had been preparing this calf in expectation of the day that his son would return to his waiting arms. Likewise, our Father has gifts that He has stored up for us in expectation of our receiving His love and mercy.

Read Psalm 145:8 and fill in the blank.
The Lord is gracious and full of compassion, slow to _____ and _____ in _____.

This story is the perfect illustration of the compassion and mercy that our heavenly Father extends toward us. When we sin He is not waiting to beat us with a large stick, He is not angry or unforgiving, nor does He reject us. He longs for our return and waits patiently with open arms and a compassionate and merciful heart for His repentant child.

Many of us could probably better relate to the older brother in the story of the prodigal. We've lived in the Father's house yet never received nor understood the depth of love our Father has for us. *Read Luke 15:25-32.*

Though the older son had remained living in his father's house, working in his father's fields and being obedient to his father, he didn't have a revelation of the love his father had for him. His father loved him dearly and would have given him anything that he had asked of him. But because he didn't understand the love of his father, he never asked. So when he saw his father freely forgiving his younger brother for his transgressions, he became angry and unforgiving.

When we fail to understand the unconditional love of our heavenly Father, we will not have eyes to see the love He has for the sinner. When our brothers and sisters in Christ fall short or offend us; we will not be able to love them unconditionally nor extend mercy to them. The older brother felt that the father should have the same attitude as he did. He wasn't willing to extend mercy or compassion toward his wayward brother.

When we are not walking in the revelation of God's love, we will expect others to earn our love based on their behavior toward us. In the older brother's eyes, the younger brother had not earned the father's love. However, due to his strict obedience, he felt that he deserved the father's love.

We are told in the Word of God that our salvation is a free gift of God's grace. We didn't do anything to earn His love, and we don't have to continue to earn His love to keep it.

*Read **Ephesians 2:4-5** and fill in the blanks.*
"But God, who is _____ in mercy, because of His _____ _____ with which He loved us, even when we were dead in trespasses, made us alive together with Christ (by grace you have been saved)."

> *Freely you have received, freely give.*
> *Matthew 10:8*

Since God does not require us to do anything to earn His love, we shouldn't demand our spouse, our children, our brother's and sister's in Christ, or anyone for that matter, to strive to earn our love. Love is a free gift. Freely you have received…freely give.

God's agape love never fails, and it never quits on us even though we may quit on Him. God says in His Word that He will never leave us or forsake us. His desire is that we would never give up on our love toward our spouse, family members, friends or the body of Christ. In the story of *Skandalon*, Zoe chose to walk away from the Lord. But throughout the story, we see the Father working in her life to draw her back to Him. He never left her, and He never gave up on her.

The Apostle Paul could certainly understand the mentality of the older brother. He'd lived a legalistic life of doing works in an effort to please God. He'd even committed his life to placing Christians in prison to fulfill what he mistakenly thought was the Father's heart. However, on the road to Damascus he had an encounter that changed his life forever. He came to know, by faith, the love of his Father. His great desire was that the body of Christ would understand how deeply and dearly loved we are.

We have to receive this love by faith. We can't be led by our feelings nor how we view our circumstances. Many are deceived into thinking that because they are going through a trial,

God must be angry with them. Nothing could be farther from the truth. We are promised that we will experience difficult times while living on this earth. But, God promises that He walks with us through the storms and fiery trials *(Isaiah 43:2)*.

Skandalon
Zoe hummed softly as she made her way home from work. An old familiar tune kept bubbling
up in her spirit. She sang aloud as the words came flooding back to her remembrance.
Into my heart, into my heart,
Come into my heart, Lord Jesus; Come in today, come in to stay;
Come into my heart, Lord Jesus.
She wiped away tears falling on her cheeks as she sang the hymn over and over again.
And then suddenly, she heard a voice rumble up out of her spirit. It was distinctive and authoritative
yet filled with compassion.
Page 322

Let's close out today with one last Scripture.

Please read Isaiah 49:14-16 and fill in the blanks.
But Zion said, "The Lord has forsaken me, and my Lord has forgotten me."
"Can a woman forget her nursing child, and not have compassion on the son of her womb?
Surely they may forget, yet I will not _____ _____. See, I have inscribed
you on the palms of My hands; your walls are continually before Me."
In this passage, what did Zion accuse the Lord of doing? _____
_____

God compared Himself and the love He had for Zion (*the Church*) to a woman's love for her nursing child. I can't think of anything more moving or precious than when I witnessed my daughter's love for her newborn babies nursing at her breast. I watched her well up with tears, overwhelmed by the love she had for her babies.

Verse 16 says that God has inscribed you on the palms of His hands. He loves you so much that your image is permanently tattooed on the palm of His hands. You are loved, adored, cherished and accepted by Him. You are continually before Him. He thinks about you all of the time. Your face never leaves His mind. He'll never leave you, forsake you or forget you. Rest in the love He has for you.

Day 3

Beloved, if God so loved us, we also ought to love one another. 1 John 4:11

LOVE DEBT

Read Roman 13:8-10 and fill in the blanks.

Owe no one anything except to _____ one another, for he who loves another has fulfilled the _____. For the commandments, "You shall not commit adultery," "You shall not murder," "You shall not steal," "You shall not bear false witness," "You shall not covet," and if there is any other commandment, are all summed up in this saying, namely, "You shall _____ your neighbor as _____." Love does no _____ to a neighbor; therefore _____ is the fulfillment of the _____.

It is God's desire that love would motivate us to action. We are called to be doers of the Word and not hearers only. It is one thing to study about love; it is yet another thing to love someone else as much as you love yourself. In the above Scripture, we are

> *But be doers of the word, and not hearers only, deceiving yourselves.*
> *James 1:22*

exhorted to consider loving others as if it were a debt to be paid. When we love others unselfishly, considering them more than we consider our own needs or desires, we fulfill the law.

This law of radical, unselfish love is referred to as the royal law by James *(James 2:8)*. It is the law of the Kingdom of God. When we seek to walk according to the royal law of love, we are seeking first the Kingdom. Our King is the King of love. His law is to love in action; to reach out to others in love when it is inconvenient. To love when the person you are called to love is virtually unlovable, and when you feel they are unworthy of your love. The King of love reached out in His love to rescue us from eternal damnation when we were unworthy of His love. We are called to be filled with compassion and good-will toward others even when they do not treat us with the same expression of love. The royal law requires that we forgive those who have hurt or offended us; even those who would wish to do us bodily harm *(Luke 23:34)*.

*Please read **1 John 2:3-5**. Everywhere you see the word commandments, replace it with the word love.*

Now by this we know that we know Him, if we keep His _____. He who says, "I know Him," and does not keep His _____ is a liar, and the truth is not in him. But whoever keeps His word, truly the love of God is perfected in him. By this we know that we are in Him.

Our love towards others is an outward sign of our Christian maturity as well as a demonstration of our love and allegiance to the King of love. It is an act of obedience to the Word of God and His command to love.

*Read **1 John 4:8** and fill in the blanks.*
He who does not _____ does not _____ God, for God is _____.

We can all agree that God is the greatest force there is. He is all-powerful and almighty. There is no greater power that operates in the heavens or on the earth. If God is love, can we then also conclude that there is no greater force on this earth than love? When we choose to walk in the God-kind of love, we are aligning ourselves up with His perfect will, His power, His might and His ability to overcome every opponent that would stand in opposition to us. Love places us in perfect agreement with God and under His protection. Nothing can withstand God. Therefore, nothing can withstand love. God is love, and He never fails.

> Love never fails.
> 1 Corinthiams 13:8

We must choose to love others the way God does which means we must not be moved by how we feel because our feelings can lie to us. God's love operating in and through us is a determined decision on our part to love those we deem to be unlovable. When we decide to love others unconditionally, God promises us that we will not fail, because His love never fails.

*Read **Romans 5:5** and fill in the blanks.*
"...the love of God has been _____ out in our hearts by the _____ _____ who was given to us."

In other words, when you call upon the grace of God to love an individual unconditionally, God will enable you to do so. However, you must make a choice. We know with certainty that we are capable of expressing this agape love in all of our relationships.

Generally speaking, it's the people we are closest to that test us the most in our decision to walk in love. God will use our spouse, parents, wayward children, those we work with or for…to mold us into vessels that carry the sweet fragrance of His love. He uses them to perfect us in love.

If we choose to be willing and obedient to the model of Christ' selfless love, we learn how to give of ourselves unselfishly, how to die to our rights while we place the desires of others above our own. We learn to love imperfect individuals. And daily, we are reminded that life was not meant to be *all about me*. In return, we are blessed with lasting, fulfilling relationships with whom we can grow in God and enjoy sweet fellowship while sharing our lives, hopes, dreams, fears, failures, and joys.

Skandalon

"Romans 5:5 reminds us that God's love has been poured out in our hearts by the Holy Spirit. Therefore, I have the ability and capacity living within me to love just as He loves. I can love because Love, with a capital L, lives in me. First John 4:8 says that God is love. If He is love and He lives in me, then it stands to reason that I can love others just as I am loved by Him. Loving others is so very important to God because love is the essence of who He is. We need to be praying to have His love flowing through us more than we pray for great assignments or spiritual gifts because, without His love as the foundation, these are nothing."
Zoe got lost in the message. She thought about Grandma Abby and how she'd neglected her in the last few months of her life because she'd been engrossed in her self-centered lifestyle. She'd gotten so wrapped up in her loss that she hadn't reached out to her grandma. She thought about Michael and how he'd loved her unconditionally. He'd continued to love her even when she'd strayed from her marriage and her faith. He was an example to her of Christ's love. She found it unbearable to think that she'd squandered such a love. She glanced down at Barbara, who was beaming from ear to ear as she listened to her pastor. Today was a special day for Barbara, having her husband and children in church with her. Barbara had tried so many times to reach out to her in love, and Zoe had turned her down coldheartedly. She was thankful God's love had mended the gap between them.
Page 228

Read *1 Corinthians 13:4–7. Let's examine this passage.*

Love suffers long and is kind! To suffer long means that we trust in the Lord and His process as He works in our life, our spouse's life, our children's lives and in the lives of our family and friends.

It is the choice to be patient and to bear or endure pain, trouble, and hardship without complaining or losing self-control. As Christ followers, we are not to be easily provoked or angered by others. We must choose to respond in love to those who offend, upset and provoke us, instead of reacting in anger and retaliation.

There are no perfect people in the world, including yourself (*sorry to disappoint*). Just as we'd appreciate others to be patient with us, we need to be patient with those who do not always meet our expectations.

Love waits patiently for promises to come to pass. It is kind even when the normal response to a situation would be anger. It is gentle, caring and gracious. Love trusts God to work His good in every circumstance.

Agape love does not envy!

*Please read **1 Corinthians 14:1** and fill in the blank.*
Pursue love, and _____ spiritual gifts, but especially that you may prophesy.

The word *desire* in this passage is the Greek word *zeloo*[65]. This is the same Greek word translated as *envy* in **1 Corinthians 13:4**. It means to be zealous for, to burn with desire, to pursue ardently, to desire eagerly or intensely. Therefore, when we allow envy to take hold of our hearts, we are allowing our hearts to burn intensely for something that God has not meant for us to have.

Those who walk in the God-kind of love are not afraid to help others reach their highest potential and are pleased when others are promoted, favored and honored. They do not desire or covet the possessions, spiritual gifts or talents of others but rejoice with them in their blessings because they understand that blessings, favor, and possessions are dependent on God, and He alone decides what we need and when we need it.

Agape love does not parade itself! Christ's love in us should motivate us to turn the conversation to focus on the achievements of others, drawing them into the conversation and shining the light on them instead of thinking that we need to be the center of attention at all times.

Agape love is not puffed up!

*Read **1 Peter 5:5** and fill in the blanks.*
Likewise you younger people, submit yourselves to your elders. Yes, all of you be _____ to one another, and be _____ with

_____, for "God _____ the _____, but gives _____ to the humble."
Who does God resist? _____

I don't know about you, but I never want to give the Father an opportunity to resist or stand against me! I need all of the grace I can get on a daily basis.

The God-kind of love is not prideful or arrogant. It is spiritually healthy to have a genuine assessment of our capabilities, as well as shortcomings. Love that is puffed up is dictatorial and domineering (*my way or the highway*). When we are prideful, we have an exaggerated opinion of our self and believe that others would not be able to function properly without us. However, agape love understands that everything that we are, and all that we have, including any spiritual gifts or qualities, is solely because of God's grace.

Agape love does not behave rudely! Instead, it displays good manners and is courteous in every situation, even when provoked by someone who is being rude. It is polite even when patience is tested, and it does not get its way. It behaves mannerly and listens when others are speaking. It does not make crude jokes about other's race, appearance or mannerisms. God's love enables us to extend the same grace to others that He so freely gives to us. Living in this age of modern technology and the Internet, we must be careful of the things we post online without regard of those who'll be viewing it. We may not agree with someone else's decisions or lifestyles, but we are still commanded to demonstrate Christ's love to them.

Agape love does not seek its own! If I am walking in the love of Christ, I fully realize that I am my brother's keeper! Christ's example to us was to lay down His life so that we might have eternal life. If I am choosing love, I will think of others needs over and above my own. Agape love is not seen in a *"here I am"* person but is ever present in a *"there you are"* person. Love that does not seek its own seeks to be a blessing in someone else's life rather than expecting to be blessed by others. When we walk in this love, we understand that we are not the center of our world. God is!

*Read **1 Corinthians 10:24** and fill in the blanks.*
Let no one seek his _____, but each one the _____ well–being.

Love is not provoked! Agape love is not irritable, touchy, rough or hostile, but is instead, graceful under pressure. The love of God demands that we are to be ruled by the Spirit of God and not by fleshly emotions. Love does not try to start an argument but will seek to be the one who is quick to put out a spark before it turns into a fire. It is slow to speak and slow to anger but quick to repent and quick to obey!

*Read **Luke 6:27-28** and fill in the blanks.*
"But I say to you who hear: Love your _____, do _____ to those who _____ you, _____ those who _____ you, and _____ for those who spitefully use you.

Love thinks no evil!

Agape love does not keep an account or list of offenses and wrongs. It willingly lets go of the past. It frees others to be imperfect and make mistakes. Mature love does not meditate on anger, resentment or disappointment because of unmet expectations, but strives to be loving and forgiving. When we are living the love life, we quickly forget when others hurt, disappoint, offend, or make us angry. Love causes us to think the best of everyone and believe that their motives are pure.

Love does not rejoice in iniquity but rejoices in the truth!

*Please read **Proverbs 17:9** and fill in the blanks.*
He who _____ a transgression seeks love, but he who _____ a matter separates friends.

The God-kind of love does not find satisfaction in the shortcomings of others and will not spread or listen to an evil report about them. It would never uncover the sins of others. Instead, it covers the sins of others as if they were their own. It speaks the truth of God's Word over others instead of talking and rehearsing their faults. The one who chooses love is too busy examining his/her own heart to be concerned with everyone else's.

Love bears all things, believes all things, hopes all things, endures all things! Those who choose to live a life of love will take Christ at His Word. They believe that if God said it, He will do it! They understand that He is not a God who can or will lie to them. Love trusts and has faith in His ability and willingness to work for the good in every situation. It hopes even in the midst of impossible circumstances, knowing that God is in control. It believes that He can do exceedingly abundantly above all that we can think or imagine. Love never let's go of God!

Let's agree to begin to allow this Scripture passage to be the measuring stick in our relationships to determine how well we are walking in love with one another.

*Read **1 John 3:16-18** and fill in the blanks.*
By this we know love, because He laid down His life for us. And we also ought to lay down our _____ for the _____. But whoever has this world's goods,

and sees his brother in need, and shuts up his heart from him, how does the love of God abide in him? My little children, let us not love in word or in _____*, but in* _____ *and in truth.*

In the above verse, we are commanded to lay down our lives for the brethren. Please list below all who you'd consider to be your brethren. _____

_____

_____

_____

May I just say that the brethren can include anyone with whom we come into contact?
What do you think it means in this Scripture when it says we are not to love in word or in tongue?

_____

_____

_____

Think of the most unlovable person you know (we generally all know that one person) and list a few ways that you could demonstrate the love of God to them this week.

_____

_____

_____

_____

_____

_____

_____

_____

Day 4

By this all will know that you are My disciples, if you have love for one another." John 13:35

THE POWER OF LOVE

One day in prayer the Lord spoke something profound to me, "My love is My power. If You want power, seek more love."

*Read **1 Corinthians 13:13** and fill in the blanks.*
And now abide faith, hope, love, these three; but the _____ *of these is*
_____ *.*

There will be a day in the life of every Christian when faith and hope will no longer be needed *(1 Corinthians 13:10-12)*. However, love is eternal. We will always need love. Love has the power to outlast all that we see with our natural eyes.

*Let's look at **Ephesians 3:16-20**. We'll examine it verse by verse. Look at **Ephesians 3:16** and fill in the blanks:*
That He would grant you, according to the _____ *of His glory, to be strengthened with* _____ *through His Spirit in the inner man,*

The word *might* is the Greek word *dynamis*. It is from this Greek word that we get the English word dynamite (*we studied this word in an earlier lesson*). It is defined as miraculous power; ability; abundance, mighty work, strength and the working of a miracle.

Not only will God grace you to walk in love, but also there is a dynamic enabling power available to the believer who chooses to walk in love. Let me remind you that God is love. Therefore, the greatest power that exists is Love, and He resides in you. And Love never fails. His love will empower you to stand in the midst of opposition, to love those who do not love you in return, and to overcome bad habits and strongholds in your life. His love will empower you to heal the sick, deliver the oppressed and speak words of life to those who are weary.

Skandalon

Her mind then turned to her friend Carol. She had told Zoe
how she'd often prayed for her even before they'd become friends. Carol was certainly a demonstration of
God's love to her. She was a person who loved selflessly, even when love wasn't reciprocated in return. She
silently thanked God for her friend. She was teaching her, by example, so much about love and forgiveness and
dealing with tragedy.
Page 328

*Read **1 John 4:10** and fill in the blanks.*
In this is _____, not that we loved God, but that He _____
us and sent His Son to be the propitiation for our sins.

We know that it was love that empowered Christ to go to the cross, enabling Him to endure the suffering and the shame of bearing our sins. Everything God does flows from an outpouring of His love.

When Paul wrote the book of Ephesians, there were no chapter or verse divisions. So we see in the next few verses that proceed in Chapter 4, Paul continues his exhortation regarding the subject of love. *Look at **Ephesians 4:1-3** and fill in the blanks.*

I, therefore, the prisoner of the Lord, beseech you to _____ _____
of the calling with which you were called, with all lowliness and gentleness, with longsuffering,
_____ with one another in _____, endeavoring to keep the
_____ of the Spirit in the bond of peace.

*Now please read **Psalm 133:1-2** and fill in the blanks.*
Behold, how good and how pleasant it is for brethren to dwell together in _____!
It is like the precious _____ upon the head, running down on the beard, the beard
of Aaron, running down on the edge of his garments.

Did you notice the one word both of these verses had in common? What was it? _____

The oil represents the anointing which is God's power to flow through the life of the believer.

Aaron was the first High Priest. The oil being poured on him represents him being anointed or empowered for service to the Lord. When we walk in love, we are empowered for service. When the Body of Christ flows together in unity (*love*), there is the increased ability for the anointing to flow and the miraculous to happen.

Unity flows from the believer who is empowered by love. Satan desires to keep us from walking in unity because he knows that unity flows from love, and love is our power source. It is why he will do all that he can to stir up discord and strife in the Body of Christ. When the flow of love ceases in your life, you will notice a decrease in the anointing to do what God has called you to do.

*Read **Ephesians 3:17** and fill in the blanks:*
That Christ may dwell in your hearts through faith; that you, being _____ *and*
_____ *in love.*

To walk in the power of love, we must be rooted and grounded in love. How does that happen, you might ask? We become rooted and grounded as we immerse ourselves in the study of love just as we are doing in this week's lessons. We need to have a firm understanding of what it means to walk in the God-kind of love. Memorization of Scriptures about love will also cause us to become rooted and grounded. I believe that God has shown me to pray daily to have my thoughts and actions filtered through His love. Our spirit man should be so filled with love that we are more inclined to respond in love than to react in anger or offense. We must also guard our heart against judging others, becoming easily offended and harboring unforgiveness.

*Read **Ephesians 3:18-19** and fill in the blanks:*
May be able to comprehend with all the saints what is the _____ *and*
_____ *and* _____ *and* _____ *— to know*
the love of Christ which passes knowledge; that you may be filled with all the _____
of God.

Our minds are unable to comprehend the depths of God's love for us without a supernatural revelation. We receive it by faith as the Holy Spirit makes us aware of the depths of the Father's love toward us.

The word *fullness*[66] in the above Scripture is the Greek word *pleroma*. It means full number, full complement; full measure, copiousness, plentitude; and that which has been completed. The word describes a ship with a full cargo and crew or a town with no empty house. The word strongly emphasizes fullness and completion.

*Read **Ephesians 3:20** and fill in the blank:*
Now to Him who is able to do exceedingly abundantly above all that we ask or think, according to the _____ *that works in us.*

If you are a believer in Christ, the power of love is already at work in you. The more you receive and walk in His power (*love*), the more He is able to do in and through you.

The more proficient you are at walking in love, the more invincible you become to the

> *Then He said to them all, "If anyone desires to come after Me, let him deny himself, and take up his cross daily, and follow Me.*
> *Luke 9:23*

traps and snares of the enemy to cause you to become offended or have your feelings hurt. You'll find it natural to be slow to anger and quick to forgive.

So how do you become proficient at walking in the God-kind of love? You deny yourself, take up your cross, follow Christ, and die daily to your flesh (*1 Corinthians 15:31*). The word *deny*[67] used in *Luke 9:23*, means to forget one's self, lose sight of one's self and one's own interests.

You must also be quick to repent and ask for forgiveness when you have not acted or responded out of love. Repent means to turn around or to change. True repentance involves three things: acknowledging the truth once it is revealed to you; admitting you were wrong which is confessing your sin, bringing with it the responsibility to change; and following through by adjusting your actions or doing things differently.

*Read **Ephesians 5:1-2** and fill in the blanks.*
Therefore be _____ *of God as dear children. And walk in* _____, *as Christ also has loved us and given Himself for us, an offering and a sacrifice to God for a sweet-smelling aroma.*

We are to imitate Christ's example of love; giving of ourself as a sacrifice for others. Everything that Christ did was motivated by love. Therefore, everything we do should also be motivated by love. Love should motivate us to walk in obedience to the Word. It motivates us to be godly spouses, children, parents, etc. Our motivation for doing our job to the best of our ability is love. When we allow love to be our primary motivation (*both our love for God and others*), our lives will become a sweet-smelling aroma. We won't need to proclaim to the world that we are Christians, they'll know it by our love.

Anything that we do that is not motivated by love or is not an outflow of God's love is worthless and profits nothing and is a manifestation of the flesh and not of the Spirit.

How disappointing it would be to stand before the Father only to discover that all of our works were for nothing because love did not motivate them.

Let our prayer be that God would wash us in His love. That we would know the width and length and depth and height of His love for us so that it might be manifested in our lives to our families, friends and a lost and dying world. May others know us by His love.

Day 5

And to love Him with all the heart, with all the understanding, with all the soul, and with all the strength, and to love one's neighbor as oneself, is more than all the whole burnt offerings and sacrifices." Mark 12:33

GOING DEEPER IN LOVE

Read 1 Corinthians 14:1 and fill in the blanks.

_____ *love, and* _____ *spiritual gifts, but especially that you may prophesy.*

We are exhorted to pursue love, yet many in the Body of Christ pursue spiritual gifts and the supernatural (*there's nothing wrong with either of these*) over and above their pursuit of love.

The Message Bible interprets this Scripture this way: *Go after a life of love as if your life depended on it – because it does.* Can you imagine how differently we'd view loving others if we truly believed our life depended on it? If we could peer into the spiritual realm and see the doors we open to the enemy when we refuse to walk in love…we'd love as if our life

---

Skandalon

"Sir, I beg your forgiveness, but I don't think this guy is going to break too easily. He's sold out. He stands against temptation by the power of the Holy Spirit. He understands and walks in his authority as a believer. He knows who he is in Christ and is obedient to Jehovah's word. He seeks Christ for direction on a daily basis. But our biggest problem is that he understands the power of love. We've tried everything we could think of, used every weapon imaginable, including the loss of his child and the divorce from his wife. We've even tried getting him hooked on television programs that would give us a foothold in his life, but the Holy Spirit revealed our strategy. How can we fight against such a strong follower of Jehovah?"

Page 339

---

depended on it!

*Read **1 Peter 1:22** and fill in the blanks.*
Since you have purified your souls in obeying the truth through the Spirit in _____
love of the brethren, love one another _____ with a
_____ heart...

This Scripture says that we are to love others sincerely, fervently and with a pure heart.

Anupokritos is the Greek word that translates into our English word *sincere*[68]. It means that we are to love without hypocrisy or pretense. In modern-day language, we could say – "just be real." Our love should flow from a heart that loves others because we know how much God loves them. I find that it's easier to love sincerely when I remind myself that Christ died for the one I'm seeking to love. I've also found that the more I pray for God to bless those who are difficult to love, the easier it is to love them.

When we love from a sincere heart, we won't speak kindly to a person when face to face yet speak slanderously or hatefully behind their backs (*that's a backstabber ya'll*). We'll be the same whether in or out of their presence.

The next word I'd like to look at is the word *fervently*[69]. This word means exhibiting or marked by great intensity of feeling, and having or showing very strong feelings. The Greek word comes from a verb which means to *stretch out the hand*. Isn't that the perfect word picture of what Christ did for us? He demonstrated how we are to love fervently by stretching out His hands on the cross and dying for our sins. Love will often stretch us beyond our comfort zone. It will challenge us to love those whom we'd rather not even give the time of day. We'll be stretched to love when it's inconvenient and uncomfortable.

> *Husbands, love your wives, just as Christ also loved the church and gave Himself for her, that He might sanctify and cleanse her with the washing of water by the word...*
> Ephesians 5:25-26

We are also called to love from a pure heart or a heart that is right before God. This word *pure*[70] means without blemish, clean, and undefiled. We can only love others in sincerity and fervently when our hearts are pure before God. The enemy will do all that he can to contaminate our hearts. Through sin, wounds of the past and situations that are a cause for offense, we can be tempted to withhold love. But when our hearts are daily washed by the water of the Word, when we seek forgiveness and healing of heart wounds, we can then love from a pure heart.

Please read *Luke 10:25-37*. This story is the perfect illustration of what it means to love sincerely and fervently from a pure heart.

In *verse 29* of the above passage, the lawyer ask Jesus – "And who is my neighbor?"

So I ask you, "Who is your neighbor?" Who do you think Jesus is referring to when He says we are to love our neighbor as ourself? _____

_____

_____

Surely, I'm not commanded to love the terrorists, the murderers, the child molesters, as well as those who are caught up in occults and false religions? Do I have to love my boss who berates me and is so hard to work for or my coworker who talks about me and makes me look bad all the time? What about my ex-husband or my husband's ex-wife (*ouch*)? How about the politician who's views I vehemently disagree with? Yes, all of these would be considered our neighbor. Nobody said that this love walk would be easy. It wasn't easy for Christ…He gave up everything for you and me.

I believe that it's safe to assume that the *certain man* mentioned in *verse 30* was probably a Jew. It's difficult to understand the lesson of this story unless you know that Jews and Samaritans mixed together like oil and water. They didn't interact with each other, and there was almost always racial tension between them. The Samaritans were despised by the Jews and considered a lesser race.

Read 1 John 4:20-21 and fill in the blanks.
If someone says, "I love God," and _____ *his brother, he is a* _____*; for he who does not love his brother whom he has seen, how can he love God whom he has not seen? And this commandment we have from Him: that he who loves God must* _____ *his brother also.*

The Jew is robbed, left naked and dying on the side of the road. A priest, no doubt a very religious person and someone who you'd expect to act with compassion and love, passes by on the opposite side of the road. Now before *you* go getting all religious on me, think of the times when you've turned around and walked the other way, crossed the street or acted like you didn't see someone in an effort to avoid them. How many times do we go out of our way so that we won't have to take the time to speak to someone we consider to be unworthy of our attention?

He was probably in a hurry and didn't want to get involved with someone else's problems. We've all been there, done that. However, love means you will often have to get involved even when it is inconvenient. Love will often take you off of your journey and place you on the path of someone else who needs you. God will often place people in our path who need our love and attention. It's a test. Will you be selfish or pass to the next level; growing from glory to glory in your love walk?

*Hold your place in Luke and turn to **Matthew 25:31-40**. After reading this passage, fill in the blank. Inasmuch as you did it to one of the _____ of these My brethren, you did it to _____ .*

The man was half-dead. The priest was probably afraid of becoming unclean if the man died while he was tending to him. Under the Levitical law, a priest was not to go near any dead body, or he would be considered unclean *(Leviticus 21:11; Numbers 19:16)*. We will often come across those on our journey who are dead *(spiritually speaking)* or dying *(backslidden)*. Will we judge them or love them and bring them to life?

Next, a Levite comes on the scene. Notice that the priest *saw*, however, the Levite *came and looked*. The Levite came close enough that he could have touched the man, but he chose not to help, probably for many of the same reasons the priest decided not to help.

I can't help but think about our modern day culture. If we, the Church, are not careful we can become like the Priest and the Levite in our story. We can allow our religiosity to keep us from reaching out to those who do not believe like us, those who are living a sinful lifestyle and those who oppose us because of our faith. Christians have been known to use their religious beliefs as an excuse to deny love and inflict judgment. We must be careful to separate the sin from the sinner and love those whose views are in opposition to ours. But a certain Samaritan came and had compassion and showed mercy. Notice that he too was on his journey yet he took the time to help someone in need. Most likely, he was aware of the fact that this stranger was a Jew and, if the tables had been turned, would probably not have stopped to give him aid. Remember, we do not love only those who will love us in return.

> *"But if you love those who love you, what credit is that to you? For even sinners love those who love them. And if you do good to those who do good to you, what credit is that to you? For even sinners do the same."*
> Luke 6:32-33

In *Luke 10:33*, it says that the Samaritan *saw him*. I believe that what the Lord is speaking to us is that the Samaritan didn't see a Jew. He simply saw his fellow man hurting and in need, and he reached out in compassion to help him. He saw beyond the man's race, the color of his skin, and his religion. When is the last time you *saw* someone in need and reached out to help them?

Notice that he treated the stranger the way he'd have wanted to be treated in the same situation *(Matthew 7:12)*. There are several ways in which this man showed love to his neighbor.

First off, he gave his *time*. Love requires us to give of our time, but we are promised in the Word that what we give will be given back in return. We can't out give God. When we give of our time for others, it is as if we are giving of ourselves to our heavenly Father.

He *risked his life* and exposed himself to danger. He didn't think of the risk to his own life as he reached out to help a stranger. For all he knew, the robbers could have been waiting to attack him. Love comes with risk. We may be called to risk our physical life to help others (m*any missionaries have given all to answer the call to go into all the world and reach the lost)*. Most of us, however, will experience the heartache of being rejected, used and taken for granted when we risk reaching out in love to help others. Our Savior risked His life for us, and yet we rejected Him.

He carried the man to safety by taking him off the road, bandaging his wounds and taking him to a safe place to heal. Have you ever heard the saying, *"Don't shoot the wounded?"* It is what the Church has often been guilty of doing (*present company included*). We have had wounded people come into our congregations, and because they are different than we are, they don't dress the way we think they should, or they still carry some of their bad habits… we shoot them (*withhold love, or worse, we run them out of the church*). However, we need to carry these wounded souls to a safe place. We must let the Holy Spirit do the sanctifying work in their lives while we love them to wholeness.

He also gave of his *finances*. I'm sure that the oil and the wine he dumped on this fellow were not cheap. He also paid for the man to stay at the inn and receive care. There is a cost to love just as there is a risk. We may never see repayment this side of heaven, but our Father promises to reward us *(Luke 6:38)*.

The Samaritan walked while he let the man ride on his animal. Therefore, he gave of his *comfort*. Love demands that we go and do…not sit and watch. Love requires us to step out of our comfort zone.

He gave of his *possessions* – wine, oil, and bandages. What are you willing to give up so that others may see the love of Christ in you?

Lastly, this man gave of *his self* – rescuing the stranger kept him from doing what he wanted or needed to be doing. Agape love requires that we give our all. It often requires us to deny our self, our desires, our schedules, and our freedom so that we may reach out to others in need.

At the end of this story, Jesus gives us a challenge us in *verse 37* – *"Go and do likewise."*

8

Week Eight

Skandalon reading assignment: Chapters 29-33

Day 1

For those who live according to the flesh set their minds on the things of the flesh, but those who live according to the Spirit, the things of the Spirit. For to be carnally minded is death, but to be spiritually minded is life and peace. Romans 8:5-6

STRONG HOLDS IN YOUR MIND

In my life, the greatest strategy that the devil uses against me is to attack me in my mind (*I call it stinkin' thinkin'*). Of course, we know that he can also use others to attack us. He can come against us by attacking us as well as our loved ones with sickness or disease, through tragic circumstances, loss of jobs or homes, etc. However, on a day-to-day basis, most of his arrows are thrown against us by way of thoughts.

If the enemy can get to your mind, he can build a stronghold in your life that can keep you trapped, defeated and imprisoned instead of living the overcoming life that God has ordained for you.

His attack against our mind usually begins by bombarding us with a nagging thought, temptation, suspicion, doubt, fear, wondering, reasoning or a vain imagination. He knows that if he can get to your mind, and keep your mind thinking about what he wants you to dwell on, he will have you snared much like an innocent animal caught in a hunter's trap.

Look up 2 Corinthians 10:4-5 and fill in the blanks.

For the weapons of our warfare are not carnal but mighty in God for pulling down _____, *casting down* _____ *and every high thing that exalts itself against the knowledge of God, bringing every* _____ *into captivity to the* _____ *of Christ,*

The word *stronghold*[71] means a castle or fortress; anything on which one relies; the arguments and reasoning by which a disputant endeavors to fortify his opinion and defend it against his opponent. A stronghold is always based on a lie.

A stronghold is an incorrect thinking pattern that stems from believing something that is not true and certainly does not line up with the Word of God. It is a *strong hold* that the enemy has over your mind so that he might keep you in bondage. Strongholds can be built in our minds over a matter of weeks, months or years and are often difficult to tear down, especially if we are not even aware that they exist. Many strongholds began when we were children. Therefore, we think of these lies of the enemy as simply being a part of our personality. Strongholds keep us from receiving God's best in our lives.

A stronghold is like a fortress. For instance, we can think or dwell on a thought of poverty for so long that it becomes a fortress in our life. Perhaps our parents lived a life of poverty. Therefore, the enemy convinces us that we will always live a life of poverty; always struggling to make ends meet and living from paycheck to paycheck. We begin to believe in our heart that we'll always be living in the land of lack instead of believing for the blessings God promised to us in His Word.

In the above Scripture, the word *arguments*[72] is translated as imaginations in the King James Version. I like that rendering better because we can more easily understand the point Paul was trying to make. Satan places these imaginations into our mind; a seed thought. We then fertilize and water that negative thought by constantly thinking about it and thus, cause the thought to grow and mature. According to the Strongs Concordance, an argument is a reasoning that is hostile to or in opposition to the Christian faith.

I've shared that one of the greatest strongholds that I had to be set free from in my life was the stronghold that God was an unloving Father. For years, I believed the lie that He was a harsh taskmaster always looking to punish me and make me pay for my sins when, in fact, Jesus paid for my sins. This stronghold held me in such bondage. It kept me from walking in my destiny and receiving the love of my Father.

We see in the above verse that Paul is making a definite link between a stronghold and the thought life. There is a warfare going on in the spirit realm. Satan desires to have control of your thought life. And, if you are not in control of it, and you are not guarding your thoughts, he has control (*Ouch!*).

If we are to overcome these strongholds we are going to have to take captive every thought and bring it into the obedience of Christ. In other words, we have to think about what we are thinking about and measure our thoughts against the Word of God. Any thought that doesn't measure up against the Word, we must dispel and dismiss. When we are tuned into the Holy Spirit, He will also make us aware of thoughts that can lead to strongholds in our lives.

It is imperative that we know the Word of God. You cannot be a casual Christian or you will become a casualty of war.

Read John 8:32 and fill in the blanks.
And you shall _____ the truth, and the truth shall make you
_____.

Many have been known to misquote this verse by saying, "The truth will set you free." Notice, however, that the Scripture actually says that it is the truth that you *know* that sets you free.

⁂

Skandalon

Brad reached into the console of his truck and pulled out a well-worn pocket New Testament. He located a familiar scripture. "Let me read you a scripture. 'For though we walk in the flesh, we do not war according to the flesh. For the weapons of our warfare are not carnal but mighty in God for pulling down strongholds, casting down arguments and every high thing that exalts itself against the knowledge of God, bringing every thought into captivity to the obedience of Christ.'"

"Bro, I know that you know you have a real enemy. He hates you, and he hates the institution of marriage because it mirrors the relationship we are to have with Christ. I think he's doing a number on your mind trying to get you to focus on what Zoe did and your anger toward this Zach dude. You need to take those thoughts captive. You need to walk in forgiveness and get back up to that room and try to get your wife back. That's where your focus should be. Getting her back and determining whether or not that's your son."

Page 374

⁂

You must know the truth so that you can refute the lies of the enemy. We can read or hear the the Word of God. However, until we become firmly rooted and grounded in it, it will not bring freedom.

Satan has several major weapons that he uses against the mind of the believer to build a stronghold: deception, temptation, confusion, and accusation.

*Look up **John 8:44** and fill in the blanks.*
You are of your father the _____, and the desires of your father you want to do. He was a murderer from the beginning, and does not stand in the _____, because there is _____ truth in him. When he speaks a _____, he speaks from his own resources, for he is a _____ and the father of it.

So there you have it! Satan is the father of lies. He's great at lying and deceiving because he has had thousands of years to practice his trade on billions of souls.

One way that Satan will build a stronghold in your life is to deceive you into thinking that God is mad at you or that He can't possibly use you because you are flawed. Women especially tend to see themselves in a negative light because Satan has lied to them and told them that to be perfect, you must be a certain weight, dress a particular way, be in the right crowd, wear name brand shoes, and the list could go on and on. Many men, on the other hand, believe the lie that they have to have the right degree from the most prestigious university, make a certain amount of money, dress a certain way to be successful, live in the best neighborhood, etc.

Satan has convinced many of us that we are unqualified and not spiritual enough for God to love us or use us for His glory. He's built strongholds of insecurity in our minds that hold us in bondage to the lie that we have no purpose in the kingdom of God.

What lie has the enemy spoken to you? _____
_____
_____
_____
_____

*Please read **Judges 6:11-16** and answer the following questions.*
*Look at **verse 12**, where did the Angel of the Lord see Gideon?* _____
_____
_____
_____
_____

Now, take a look at ***verse 15***. *What stronghold had Satan built in Gideon's mind? Hint: how did Gideon see himself as opposed to how God saw him?* _____

_____

_____

_____

_____

According to ***verse 13***, *what do you think Satan used to erect this stronghold in Gideon's life?*

_____

_____

_____

_____

What did the Lord do to combat the stronghold in Gideon's life? (see ***verse 14****)* _____

_____

_____

_____

_____

Often, the enemy will use defeat in our lives to convince us that we are not, nor never will be, who God has called us to be. However, I hope you saw in *verses 12* and *14*, that God called Gideon a mighty man of valor even when Gideon saw himself as the least in his tribe. God chose to use Gideon to defeat the Midianites even when he saw himself as a weakling. God will never agree with the enemy or even the lies we choose to believe about ourselves. He sees us as overcomers; well able to do whatever He has called us to do.

No doubt, the adversary used men within Gideon's own tribe to speak lies into the heart of the young man. He does that to you and me as well. We often have the voices of our past ringing in our ears the lies we've heard from the lips of those who have spoken negatively into our lives.

We often think of a stronghold as being one of the big sins like pornography, adultery or addiction. However, a major stronghold can be fear, anger, pride, criticalness, rejection or control. Strongholds come in many forms.

We've also discussed in previous lessons that every temptation begins with a thought. First, the enemy will place a temptation before you. The temptation might be to have an affair, look at pornography on the computer, enter into a sexual relationship before marriage, or steal something from your office while no one is looking. The enemy deceives you into thinking that what you are doing is not wrong, that your actions are not hurting anyone, or that you can do it just one time, and no one will know or be hurt by your actions. He'll convince you that you are justified in your decision. Often, he'll even bend or twist Scriptures around in your mind to deceive you into believing that it is okay. He'll show you a worm, but behind every worm is a hook. Then, when he has deceived you into believing that it's okay, he'll tempt you into following through with the thought, and you will soon find yourself trapped in his snare *(Proverbs 7:21-23)*.

Obviously, the greatest way to overcome a temptation is never to let your mind meditate on the thought. Simply don't go there!!! You have a choice to make as to whether or not you are going to meditate on a wrong thought, which, if you do, will eventually cause you to give into it. Or, you can cast down the thought and bring it into the obedience of Christ. When we resist the enemy, sooner or later he will flee.

> *Therefore submit to God. Resist the devil and he will flee from you. Draw near to God and He will draw near to you. Cleanse your hands, you sinners; and purify your hearts, you double-minded.*
> *James 4:7-8*

We overcome strongholds by first identifying the stronghold or wrong thinking pattern. We then use the Word of God to stand against the lies of the enemy. For instance, I had to study what the Bible said about God's love for me and His grace that has been poured out for me to counter the lie that God was always ready to beat me over the head with a stick when I did something wrong.

Confession and repentance are an important part of breaking strongholds. We must confess the lie and ask forgiveness for believing the lies of the enemy and allowing them to take precedence over the truth of God's Word. We forgive those who may have played a role in the forming of the stronghold. My mother and father played a huge part in the formation of the stronghold in my life. I had to realize that God did not punish the way they did nor would He reject me because I failed to do what He asked of me. Therefore, I had to forgive them and ask God to forgive me for believing the lie that He was like them.

We renounce the sin and close any doors that we have opened to the enemy because of the sin. For instance, if before becoming a Christian, we believed the lie that it's okay to have sex before marriage, we may have opened a door for the enemy to tempt us into further sexual sin like pornography or adultery. We then, using the blood of Jesus, bind the enemy and command that he depart. Finally, we ask the Holy Spirit to come in and help us to renew our mind and replace old thought patterns with the Word of God.

I have a dear friend, Krisann Nething, who has written a great book called *Walking Out Your Victory*. In it, she goes much deeper into the process of breaking free from demonic strongholds. I highly recommend this book.

Let's end today with a prayer:

Father God, set a guard about my heart. Help me to guard my heart against the temptations and deceptions of the enemy. I submit my thought life to You and ask that You, Holy Spirit, would quicken me when I am entertaining the lies of the enemy. Reveal every stronghold in my life and help me to be set free from the snares of the enemy. In Jesus' Name, Amen!

Day 2

And be renewed in the spirit of your mind... Ephesians 4:23

THE BATTLE IN YOUR MIND

We talked about this in our previous lesson, but how many of us think about what we are thinking about on a regular basis? Have you ever been in the shower or perhaps doing dishes and suddenly realized that your mind is dwelling on something it shouldn't? I have!

Skandalon

Zoe's mind was in turmoil, and her soul was filled with fear as she left the hospital. How can they have so much peace? How would I respond if anything like that happened to Amos? Oh God, I feel like I'm just getting my faith back on the right track. Please don't let anything happen to this baby. I don't think I could bear it. I don't think...

Suddenly, in her spirit, she heard a gentle whisper, and she knew it was the voice of God.

"Be still and know that I am God."

Page 344

Read **Romans 8:5** *and fill in the blanks.*
For those who live according to the _____ *set their* _____ *on the things of the flesh, but those who live according to the* _____, *the things of the* _____.

The Bible makes it clear that we are to guard our thoughts. I once heard a saying that has stuck with me:

Guard your thoughts because they become your words.
Guard your words because they become your actions.
Guard your actions because they become your character.

Guard your character because it determines your destiny.

Our thoughts bear fruit for good or evil. They affect us as well as others in a negative way or a positive way.

People who dwell on judgmental, negative, fearful, critical, revengeful, angry or discouraging thoughts are going to display these same characteristics or fruit in their lives. Have you ever awakened with a negative thought that set the mood for your entire day?

> *I will meditate on Your precepts,*
> *And contemplate Your ways.*
> Psalm 119:15

On the other hand, people who dwell on the things of the Spirit of God such as cheerful, merciful, loving, peaceful and forgiving thoughts, will display these characteristics or fruit in their lives.

Many of our bad habits are simply a result of a poor thought life. An undisciplined thought life produces bad habits. Those bad habits can hinder you from fulfilling your destiny.

Read Joshua 1:8 and fill in the blanks.
This Book of the Law shall not depart from your mouth, but you shall _____ in it _____ and _____, that you may _____ to _____ according to all that is written in it. For then you will make your way _____, and then you will have good _____.

The word *meditate*[73] is the Hebrew word *hagah*. It means to reflect, to moan, to mutter; to ponder or to contemplate something as one repeats words. Jewish culture believed that to meditate upon the Scriptures meant to repeat them in a soft, droning sound while utterly abandoning outside distractions. We have to learn to meditate on the Scriptures in such a way that outside thoughts cannot come into our mind and distract us from what we know to be true. I can remember times when I have overcome fear in this manner.

As born again children of God we have a command from God to guard our thoughts. We are to think like God. The Word declares that we have the mind of Christ. Therefore, we have the ability to think like Him. Our thoughts, for the most part, should be thoughts that are positive, and cheerful, and they should never be opposed to the Word of God.

If you want to be successful and always growing in your walk with God, *you* have to conquer your thought life or the enemy will. Notice that *Joshua 1:8* makes it very clear that what you meditate on is what is going to come out of your mouth.

Read Daniel 1:8 and fill in the blanks.

Who made the decision to exclude Daniel from the delicacies of the king's table? _____

Why did he feel that he should be excluded from the delicacies of the king's table? _____
_____

Our thoughts can defile us. Other than God, no one can hear your thoughts. Therefore, you must be the one to stand against them. Rest assured, God's grace is well able to help you overcome negative thought patterns (*Hebrews 4:16*).

*Read **Psalm 101:3** and fill in the blanks.*
I will _____ nothing _____ before my _____ ;
I hate the work of those who fall away; It shall not cling to me.

As I've said before, what we gaze upon can influence our thoughts. We must be selective in what we watch on television, view in magazines, read in books, and look at on the Internet.

Your thoughts can determine how you view others. For instance, if you constantly dwell on the negative character traits of your husband, (*he doesn't put the toilet paper on the right way; he never takes out the trash; he doesn't show me enough affection*) your attitude toward him will probably not be very loving.

On the other hand, if you choose to dwell on the good qualities of your spouse instead of what you think he or she is doing wrong, it can change your outlook as well as your relationship.

When we meditate continually on negative, unholy, impure thoughts, we then begin to act on the thoughts that are dominating our mind.

Much of the time we allow rambling thoughts to overtake our minds. We often miss what God is speaking to us because we haven't learned to keep our mind at rest and our thoughts under control.

*Read **Romans 12:2** and fill in the blanks.*
And do not be conformed to this world, but be _____ by the
_____ of your _____ that you may prove what is
that good and acceptable and perfect will of God.

Our minds are renewed as we focus on God and His Word as well as not allowing our mind to wander into negative, unproductive thinking. God has given us the ability to guard our thought life. We do not have to submit to the whim of our every thought. No! We have

THE BATTLE IN YOUR MIND

to bring our minds under the subjection of Christ. If it doesn't glorify Him or the Kingdom of God, we probably ought not to be dwelling on it.

*Read **2 Timothy 1:7** and fill in the blanks.*
For God has not given us a spirit of fear, but of power and of love and of a _____ _____.

The words *sound mind*[74] is a combination of the Greek words *sos*, which means *safe*, and *phren*, which means *the mind*. A sound mind means safe-thinking. The word denotes good judgment, disciplined thought patterns, and the ability to understand and make right decisions. It includes the qualities

> *Be anxious for nothing, but in everything by prayer and supplication, with thanksgiving, let your requests be made known to God; and the peace of God, which surpasses all understanding, will guard your hearts and minds through Christ Jesus.*
> Philippians 4:6-7

of self-control and self-discipline. We must be self-controlled in our thinking.

When we allow our minds to run amuck, we can easily find ourselves agitated, fearful and at a loss for peace. God's Word tells us that we are to be anxious for nothing. We are to let God's peace guard our heart and mind. We do this by bringing all of our anxious thoughts to God in prayer, staying focused on His promises and thanking Him for working them out in our lives.

*Read **Isaiah 26:3** and fill in the blanks.*
You will keep him in perfect _____, *whose* _____ *is stayed on You, because he trusts in You.*

The Hebrew word for *peace*[75] is *shalom*, and it means completeness, wholeness, health, welfare, safety, perfectness, harmony, soundness, tranquility; and the absence of agitation or discord. Who wouldn't want to have a life like that?

If you desire peace in your life, you will have to be diligent which means careful, steady and consistent effort. You can't retrain your thought life in one day. It takes working on it moment-by-moment, hour-by-hour, and day-by-day. However, the reward is a lifestyle of peace. You will also have to be determined. It will often seem like nothing is changing, but you can't get tired and quit. God showed me that it takes discipline on my part to think about my thoughts on a regular basis so that I can retrain myself to think as He thinks. Just as a soldier trains for war, we must train our mind to think the way God thinks.

For most of my life, a spirit of anxiety has plagued me, which is the total opposite of walking in peace. I would feel fearful, have sudden rapid heart palpitations and panic attacks for no real reason at all. As I have learned to keep my mind fixed on Christ, on His Word and His promises – I have seen the anxiety disappear.

Every morning, as soon as I am consciously awake, I try to fix my thoughts on the Lord; offering up a prayer of thanksgiving for the day. Before I go to sleep at night, I thank Him for His blessings, ask forgiveness for my sins and trust any problems I have into His hands. During the day, I try to think about what I am thinking about.

A surrendered mind takes commitment. Let's commit today to make Jesus the Lord of our thought life. If you do that, you've won a major victory over the enemy.

Day 3

He who guards his mouth preserves his life, but he who opens wide his lips shall have destruction.
Proverbs 13:3

POWER OF THE SPOKEN WORD

Please read **Genesis 1** *and fill in the blank.*
There is a common thread or word spoken throughout the creation event. Based on today's lesson, can you guess what that common word is? _____ (Hint: look at **verses 3, 6, 9, 11, 14, 20, 24, 26, 28, and 29.***)*

First, we see that God *said*. We then see that what He called forth into being came forth just as He spoke it. Your words have the same power. You might not be able to create a star or a galaxy, but your words have the power to create good or evil. They

> *He sends out His command to the earth;*
> *His word runs very swiftly.*
> *Psalm 147:15*

have the power to create life or death. They have the power to change your negative situation into a positive one.

Read **Genesis 1:26** *and fill in the blanks.*
Then God said, "Let Us make man in _____ _____ _____, according to _____ _____; let them have _____ over the fish of the sea, over the birds of the air, and over the cattle, over all the earth and over every creeping thing that creeps on the earth."

When God created man, He created us in His image and likeness. He gave us dominion and authority. Therefore, our words have the same power and authority. We must pay attention to the words that we speak. Our words should be life-giving words that encourage and build up ourselves as well as others. Words of doubt, unbelief, fault-finding or judgmental words should never come out of our mouth. We must train our mouths to speak correctly.

Read **Hebrews 11:3** *and fill in the blanks.*
By faith we understand that the _____ were framed by the _____

of _____, so that the things which are seen were not made of things which are visible.

Creation began when God spoke the Word. Man was created by God when He spoke the Word. The words that we speak have creative power.

*Read **Hebrews 4:12** and fill in the blanks.*
For the word of God is _____ and _____, and sharper than any two-edged sword, piercing even to the division of soul and spirit, and of joints and marrow, and is a discerner of the thoughts and intents of the heart.

God's Word is living and powerful. Let's look at these two words. First, the Greek word for *living*[76] is the word *zao*. It means to live or breathe. The Word of God has the breath of God upon it. According to the online Blue Letter Bible, this word carries the meaning of being active, blessed, and endless in the kingdom of God. Therefore, we can say that when we speak the Word of God, it has eternal consequences. The Greek word translated as *powerful*[77] in this verse is the word *energes*. God's Word is alive and full of energy. When we speak the Word of God, it is backed by God's power and energy. How amazing is that?

*Read **Romans 10:8-10** and fill in the blanks.*
But what does it say? "The word is near you, in your _____ and in your _____" (that is, the word of faith which we preach): that if you confess with your _____ the Lord Jesus and _____ in your heart that God has raised Him from the dead, you will be saved. For with the heart one believes unto righteousness, and with the _____ confession is made unto salvation.

In order to become born again into the Kingdom of God and enter into an eternal relationship with Christ, we must first confess or speak God's Word regarding salvation. We must confess that Jesus is the Son of God, the Savior of the world who died for our sins. I want you to see this because you are in the Kingdom as a result of speaking the Word in faith. The Word has eternal consequences in your life.

*Read **Matthew 8:5-13**.* A centurion came to Jesus asking Him to heal his servant. He felt unworthy to have Jesus enter into his home so he told Him that if He would just "*say the word,*" his servant would be healed. I have always been taught that this centurion had an understanding of spiritual authority, and that is why his servant was healed. And this is probably partly true. However, I believe that the greatest revelation the centurion had was the fact that Jesus' words were filled with authority and power. We need this same revelation if we are going to use the Word of God in faith. There is an authority that we have when we speak God's Word over our situation.

*Read **Isaiah 55:11** and fill in the blanks.*
So shall My _____ be that goes forth from My mouth; it shall not return to Me _____, but it shall accomplish what I please, and it shall _____ in the thing for which I sent it.

We have a promise that when we speak God's Word over our circumstances, it will not return void, and it will accomplish what it is meant to accomplish. However, we must speak it in faith and stand until we see it fulfilled. In other words, we can't say we believe God's Word in one sentence and speak words of doubt and unbelief in the next. We have to be *all in*!

Skandalon

Michael meditated on the Scripture before answering. "Whatever I ask or desire from God, He is able to do even greater, more magnificently and brilliantly than I can even imagine in my mind, if I'll just believe Him." "That's right! And you don't have to figure it out or be able to see it with your natural eyes. You simply need to begin to see you and Zoe back together through your spiritual eyes. Begin to speak like you are back together. Begin to think about being back together. Thank God for that restoration, even when you can't see it. If God has promised it, He'll make it come to pass. Abraham called those things that were not as though they were, and he believed contrary to hope. With his natural eyes, he couldn't see how he could possibly become a father of many nations. His wife's womb was dead. But because God said He would do it, Abraham believed it as if it had already happened."

Page 354

Please understand, I'm not advocating a blab it and grab it gospel. It is the Word of God spoken in faith that brings forth results in the life of the believer. There must be balance in this teaching. For instance, I will not receive a Rolex watch simply because I repeatedly say, "I'm going to receive a Rolex watch." However, when I have a need, God's promise is to meet my needs (*2 Corinthians 9:8*). Therefore, I can stand on the Word in faith, confessing with my mouth that God will meet all of my needs. Now don't get me wrong, God will also give you the desires of your heart (*Psalm 37:4*), but He most often does this as we seek first the Kingdom and delight ourselves in Him. We can confess that God will give us the desires of our heart, but our desires must also line up with His will for our lives and be in agreement with the Word.

> *And my God shall supply all your need according to His riches in glory by Christ Jesus.*
> *Philippians 4:19*

God's Word is *spirit.* The Greek word used here is *pneuma*[78]. It refers to the Spirit of God or the spirit in general. It also means a movement of air, the breath of the nostrils or mouth, or the wind. The Spirit of God breathes on the Word of God. I believe that when we speak it out of our mouths, it is as if the Spirit of God has spoken it Himself, thus infusing it with His power, authority, and eternal purpose. He brings it to life when we speak it.

We may not always see the results immediately. Therefore, we must walk by faith as Abraham did, trusting in God to bring His Word to life.

God's spoken Word has the life-giving power to change every situation, calm every storm, bring the dead to life, heal every broken body, and deliver every lost soul. Hallelujah!

With that in mind, please pick a Scripture or Scriptures that addresses any trial, need, desire or situation you are walking through.

Write it (them) down. Put it in your own words, making it a prayer to the Father.

_____

_____

_____

_____

_____

_____

_____

_____

_____

_____

_____

_____

Day 4

There is one who speaks like the piercings of a sword, but the tongue of the wise promotes health.
Proverbs 12:18

D E A T H   A N D   L I F E   A R E   I N   Y O U R   W O R D S

Have you ever heard the saying, "Sticks and stones may break my bones, but words will never hurt me?" That is a lie that comes from the pit of you know where! Your words have the power to wound or heal.

*Read **Proverbs 18:21** and fill in the blanks.*
Death and _____ are in the power of the _____, and those who love it will eat its fruit.

Death and life are in the power of your tongue. Our words have the power to kill and destroy or to bring life and healing. Words spoken in anger can damage a soul for a lifetime. However, when we speak words that nourish the soul, we will see that person flourish; whether it be our spouse, our child or a co-worker. It's so very important to guard our tongue and not allow ourselves the luxury of lashing out in anger and frustration, spouting words that cannot be taken back before they do irreparable damage.

Think about words that were spoken over you as a child. Were they words that affirmed you and built you up or were they words that tore you down? I remember as a little girl; I had the gift of gab. I loved to talk (*still do!*). My dad would constantly tell me, "Your mouth is gonna get you into trouble." And you know what? Those words followed me into adulthood until I became a Christian and broke the stronghold of those negative words over my life. My dad had no idea the power of those words or he would have never spoken them. But the enemy used them to wreak havoc in my life for many years. I was constantly saying the wrong things, backbiting, gossiping and even lying. My words kept me in trouble!

What about you? Were there negative words spoken over you as a child? You need to break the power of those words.

Say this prayer:
Father, I break the power of the words spoken over me that I would never/always be _____
_____.

217

That is not what Your Word says about me. Your Word declares that I am… (Find a Scripture and write down what God says about you. If you are not sure of a Scripture, take a moment and ask God what He says about you. It will be the opposite of the negative words spoken over you. For instance, I might have said something like this: Lord, You fill my mouth with good things.) _____

_____

_____

_____ .

Father, thank you that I am Your child. My future is filled with hope. You have great things in store for me. In Jesus' name!

Skandalon

"Keep your mind renewed in the Word. The Holy Spirit is your strengthener. He'll help you as you take steps of faith and begin to line your thoughts and words up with God. God will make sure you can live it before you preach it to someone else. He wants you to pass this test more than you do so that you can help encourage others through your ministry. A word spoken from experiential faith is a whole lot more powerful than a word spoken from head knowledge."

Page 355

Now, don't get me wrong, there will always be times when we must discipline our children. If you are in a management position on your job, you may have to bring correction to an employee. However, it's important to remember that we are to be Christ-minded. We do not have to berate another person or speak harshly to get our point across or to bring correction. God does not speak harshly to us. It is His goodness that leads us to repentance *(Romans 2:4)*.

Look up Ephesians 4:15 and fill in the blanks.
But, speaking the _____ in _____, may grow up in all things into Him who is the head—Christ…

We can speak the truth in love. We don't have to ignore negative behavior. But we are called to guard our thoughts and our words and speak words that heal and bring life.

The book of Proverbs has much to say about the importance of the words we speak. *Read Proverbs 16:23-24 and fill in the blanks.*

The heart of the _____ teaches his _____, and adds learning to his lips. _____ words are like a honeycomb, sweetness to the _____ and _____ to the bones.

A wise person will teach his lips to speak words that heal, restore and bring life. It took me several years, but once I understood the importance of this teaching, I diligently worked at training my mouth to speak life.

*Read **Ephesians 4:29** and fill in the blanks.*
Let no _____ word proceed out of your mouth, but what is good for necessary _____, that it may impart grace to the hearers.

The word *corrupt*[79] here is the Greek word *sapros*. The word means rotten or putrefied; corrupted by one and no longer fit for use, worn out; of poor quality, bad, unfit for use or worthless. Our words can be rotten and of poor quality or they can impart grace and life.

Our words can be unfit for use. Have you ever been stuck in a room with someone who uses foul language that is so offensive to your soul? It makes you want to get away from that person as quickly as possible. On the other hand, have you been around a person who consistently speaks positive, affirming words? I find myself drawn to those types of people like a bug to a nightlight.

The word *edification* in the above Scripture, speaks of building up, much like building a house or building. We need to be speaking words that build others up; encouraging them to be the best that they can be. We need to say what God says about them instead of what we might see in the natural. For instance, your child may exhibit lazy behavior patterns. The temptation would be to call them lazy. However, according to *Ephesians 4:29*, you should speak positive, affirming words to them. Perhaps, saying something like: "You are so good at accomplishing what you set your mind to do." That's called speaking faith vision or faith talk.

Something to think about: What words have you spoken over another person today? Were they positive, affirming words or negative words? _____

_____
_____

If the words were negative, ask God to forgive you and break the power of those words. Replace the negative words with positive words over that person or situation.

Write out the affirming words that should have been spoken into this situation?

_____
_____
_____

Read Matthew 12:33-35 and fill in the blanks.
"Either make the tree good and its _____ good, or else make the tree bad and its _____ bad; for a tree is known by its _____. Brood of vipers! How can you, being evil, speak good things? For out of the abundance of the heart the _____ speaks. A good man out of the good _____ of his heart brings forth good things, and an evil man out of the evil _____ brings forth evil things."

This Scripture makes painfully clear the importance of our words and the need to guard the words that come out of our mouth. However, as we previously studied, in order to guard our mouth we must first guard our thoughts. Out of the abundance of our heart (*our thought life*), our mouth will speak. Therefore, when we find ourselves speaking negatively about another person or a situation we find ourselves in, we must ask ourselves, *what is in my heart?* The Bible says that we are known by our fruit (*Luke 6:43-44*). Others are watching and listening to everything we do and say. May they see good fruit in our lives!

The words that we speak not only affect others but they can also affect how we view our situation. If I constantly speak doubt and unbelief over my circumstances, I will walk in doubt and unbelief. It will be difficult, if not impossible, for me to walk in faith. However, when I speak faith-filled words, my walk will be filled with faith.

Negative words work against us just as God's Word works for us. Think of words like seeds that produce a harvest. If we speak God's Word over our lives, our loved ones and situations that we are walking through, we will reap a good harvest. If we speak doubt, unbelief, and negative words over our lives, our loved ones, and our situations, we will reap a harvest of weeds in our life.

*Read **Proverbs 6:2** and fill in the blanks.*
You are _____ by the words of your mouth; you are _____
by the words of your mouth.

This Scripture is powerful. Our words can be used against us by the enemy. He can use them to ensnare or trap us. The word *taken*[80] means to capture or seize. Our words can cause us to remain in bondage.

I'll never get healed…
I'll always be in debt…
He'll never change…
I've been this way all my life…I'm just so stupid, clumsy, ugly,…

This type of speaking will keep us snared in the trap of the enemy. If we don't break free, we'll never rise to be the person God has called us to be and fulfill the wonderful destiny He has for our lives.

> *There is one who speaks like the piercings of a sword, but the tongue of the wise promotes health.*
> *Proverbs 12:18*

Let's close with one more Scripture.

*Please read **Proverbs 12:14** and fill in the blanks.*
A man will be satisfied with _____ by the fruit of his _____.

I cannot emphasize the fact enough…our words can determine our destiny! They can shape our future as well as the future of our children, spouse, employee, etc. Words are powerful. Something you can do:

Get two mason jars. Put a sticky note on one of the jars that says "Negative Words." Put a sticky note on the other jar that says "Positive Words." Get a bag of black beans and a bag of white beans. Every time you say something positive put a white bean in the "Positive Words" jar. Every time you find yourself speaking negatively, put a black bean in the "Negative Words" jar. Have fun with it and get the family involved.

Day 5

Then God blessed them, and God said to them, "Be fruitful and multiply; fill the earth and subdue it; have dominion over the fish of the sea, over the birds of the air, and over every living thing that moves on the earth." Genesis 1:28

THE POWER OF SPEAKING BLESSINGS

For our last lesson (*oh my goodness, I can't believe we are almost done!*), I want us to study the power of speaking a blessing. After creating Adam and Eve, God's first act was to bless them.

*Read **Genesis 5:1-2** and fill in the blank.*
This is the book of the genealogy of Adam. In the day that God created man, He made him in the likeness of God. He created them male and female, and _____ them and called them Mankind in the day they were created.

God blessed Noah and his sons after the flood. *Read **Genesis 9:1** and fill in the blank.*

"So God _____ Noah and his sons and said to them: "Be fruitful and multiply, and fill the earth."

God blessed Abram when he called him out of his country. *Read **Genesis 12:2-3** and fill in the blanks.*

I will make you a great nation; I will _____ you and make your name great; and you shall be a _____. I will _____ those who _____ you, and I will curse him who curses you; and in you all the families of the earth shall be blessed."

Throughout the Old Testament, we see this spiritual principle in operation; God speaking a blessing over His children (*Genesis 32:24-32; 2 Samuel 7:29*).

Jesus' demonstrated the importance of blessing when He blessed the children.

*Read **Mark 10:13-16** and fill in the blank.*
Then they brought little children to Him, that He might touch them; but the disciples rebuked those who

brought them. But when Jesus saw it, He was greatly displeased and said to them, "Let the little children come to Me, and do not forbid them; for of such is the kingdom of God. Assuredly, I say to you, whoever does not receive the kingdom of God as a little child will by no means enter it." And He took them up in His arms, laid His hands on them, and _____ them.

The word "*blessed*[81]" used here is the Greek word *eulogeo*. We get our English word *eulogy* from this word. It is a combination of two words *eu*, meaning *well* or *good*. And *logos* which means *speech* or *word*. It means to speak well of, praise, extol, bless abundantly, invoke a benediction, and give thanks.

It's very important to note that Jesus' last act of ministry on earth was to bless His disciples. We are called to be like Christ. I believe God is setting a precedent for His people. We are called to speak blessings into the lives of others.

Read Luke 24:50-51 and fill in the blanks.
And He led them out as far as Bethany, and He lifted up His hands and _____ them. Now it came to pass, while He _____ them, that He was parted from them and carried up into heaven.

What does it mean to speak a blessing? The blessing is the impartation of the supernatural power of God into the life of another by the spoken word of God's delegated authority. In other words, when I speak a blessing it is as if God were speaking through me. If we are going to speak a blessing over someone else, and if that blessing is to have power – we must be people under the authority of God.

> *Finally, all of you be of one mind, having compassion for one another; love as brothers, be tenderhearted, be courteous; not returning evil for evil or reviling for reviling, but on the contrary blessing, knowing that you were called to this, that you may inherit a blessing.*
> 1 Peter 3:8-9

Moses was God's delegated authority to lead Israel out of Egypt. The Lord taught him the power of the spoken blessing. God promised that if Moses spoke the blessing, He would bless Israel.

Read Numbers 6:22-27 and fill in the blanks.
And the LORD spoke to Moses, saying: "Speak to Aaron and his sons, saying, 'This is the way you shall _____ the children of Israel. _____ to them: "The Lord _____ you and keep you; The Lord make His face shine upon you, and be

gracious to you; The Lord lift up His countenance upon you, and give you peace.'" "So they shall put My name on the children of Israel, and I will _____ them."

Notice two things about this Scripture. First, though Moses was the one to speak the blessing, it was God who would stand behind and perform the blessing. God backed Moses' words. Second, we invoke a supernatural blessing by speaking it aloud. Once a spiritual authority speaks a blessing over you in faith, you can fully expect it to manifest in your life.

When we speak blessings into the lives of others in the name of Jesus, those blessings are loosed in heaven. Jesus said in *Matthew 18:18* that, *"whatever we loose on earth will be loosed in heaven."*

The Patriarchs understood that they had legal rights in heaven. As God's children, they understood that they were not powerless, but were stewards of God's mighty power to bless and see circumstances and lives turn around for the better. Being under the authority of God and in right relationship with Him, allowed them the authority to speak blessings on His behalf.

Isaac, his wife, and sons all understood that the blessing of a father upon his first-born son had supernatural power to cause that son and his family to prosper for generations into the future. Jacob understood the blessing to be so powerful that, with the help of his mother, Rebecca, he was willing to lie, cheat, and deceive to obtain the blessing of his father. A blessing that rightfully belonged to his firstborn brother Esau. In *Genesis 27*, Jacob pretended to be his brother, Esau and was able to convince his partially-blind father to give him the blessing of the first-born.

Later, when Esau came expecting to receive his blessing, he discovered that his brother, Jacob, had already received from their father an irrevocable blessing, Scripture records the following:

"And Esau said to his father, 'Have you only one blessing, my father? Bless me – me also, O my father!' And Esau lifted up his voice and wept" (Genesis 27:38).

"So Esau hated Jacob because of the blessing with which his father blessed him, and Esau said in his heart, 'The days of mourning for my father are at hand; then I will kill my brother Jacob' (Genesis 27:41).

Why was Esau so angry and hurt over the paternal blessing being given to his brother instead of to him? He was devastated because he understood the power of a spoken blessing, especially when it comes from the father.

When we speak a blessing over someone, we are imparting God's faith vision or image of identity (*Who am I?*) and destiny (*Why am I here?*) to the heart of that person. The opposite of blessing is to curse, which is an impartation of Satan's vision or image of identity and destiny into the heart of someone. When we bless someone, we are empowering them to prosper and succeed.

If you bless your son, for instance, you empower him to prosper in every area of his life; his spiritual life with God, his physical health, his emotional well-being, his marriage, his children, his finances, his career and his ministry. If you speak curses over your son, you cripple, disable or dis-empower him from prospering in all of these same areas of life.

Though God has placed the spiritual responsibility for the family upon the father to bless his children, mothers may also speak blessings over their children. As parents, we have the power and authority to speak life or death over our children. Our words of blessing over our children have the power to convey God's blessings of healing, joy, confidence, and peace.

Many of us have experienced or witnessed the fact that children who are blessed by their parents tend to prosper in their adult lives and have healthier self-esteem. Children who were never blessed by their parents, tend to struggle more in adulthood and have poor self-esteem.

We are to bless those who persecute us.

*Read **Romans 12:14** and fill in the blanks.*
_____ *those who persecute you;* _____ *and do not* _____.

We are warned against speaking curses against even those who have persecuted us *(Matthew 5:44)*.

We can speak a blessing over our own lives. Several years ago a book came out called the Prayer of Jabez. Jabez was a man who understood the power of speaking blessings over his own life. He asked God to bless him, and God granted him what he requested.

> And Jabez called on the God of Israel saying, "Oh, that You would bless me indeed, and enlarge my territory, that Your hand would be with me, and that You would keep me from evil, that I may not cause pain!" So God granted him what he requested.
> 1 Chronicles 4:10

When we speak blessings over ourselves, we are simply getting into agreement with what God has said about us *(Ephesians 1:3)*.

So, I'd like to close out our study by praying a blessing over your life:

I extend a blessing to you. May your life destiny come to pass. May your finances, your careers, your homes, your children and your health be blessed. May God's face shine upon you and may His favor be poured out on you and your household. May his goodness rain down upon you and your family. May you know Him intimately. May His angel's surround you and your loved ones. May His peace, prosperity, wholeness, and joy fill you to the fullest. May all the days of your life be filled with the knowledge of the depths of His love for you.

In closing,
Thank you for joining me in this study. I trust that the lessons learned will stick with you for a lifetime. Be blessed!

SOURCES

[1] *Ministers - Blue Letter Bible.org   Lexicon :: Strong's G3011 – leitourgos*
http://www.blueletterbible.org/lang/lexicon/lexicon.cfm?Strongs=G3011&t=KJV

[2] *Charge – Blue Letter Bible.org   Lexicon :: Strong's H6680 - tsavah*
http://www.blueletterbible.org/lang/lexicon/lexicon.cfm?Strongs=H6680&t=KJV

[3] *Bear – Blue Letter Bible.org   Lexicon :: Strong's H5375 - nasa'*
http://www.blueletterbible.org/lang/lexicon/lexicon.cfm?Strongs=H5375&t=KJV

[4] *Ministers – Blue Letter Bible.org   Lexicon :: Strong's H8334 – sharath*
http://www.blueletterbible.org/lang/lexicon/lexicon.cfm?Strongs=H8334&t=KJV

[5] *Spirit-Filled Life Bible by Thomas Nelson, Inc., Word Wealth page 1195*

[6] *Adversary – Blue Letter Bible. Org   Lexicon :: Strong's G476 - antidikos*
http://www.blueletterbible.org/lang/lexicon/lexicon.cfm?Strongs=G476&t=KJV

[7] *Devices – Blue Letter Bible.org   Lexicon :: Strong's G3540 – noēma*
http://www.blueletterbible.org/lang/lexicon/lexicon.cfm?Strongs=G3540&t=KJV

[8] *Resist – Blue Letter Bible.org   Lexicon :: Strong's G436 – anthistēmi*
http://www.blueletterbible.org/lang/lexicon/lexicon.cfm?Strongs=G436&t=KJV

[9] *Stumble – Blue Letter Bible.org   Lexicon :: Strong's G4624 – skandalizō*
http://www.blueletterbible.org/lang/lexicon/lexicon.cfm?Strongs=G4624&t=KJV

[10] *Cares – Blue Letter Bible.org   Lexicon :: Strong's G3308 – merimna*
http://www.blueletterbible.org/lang/lexicon/lexicon.cfm?Strongs=G3308&t=KJV

[11] *Principalities – Blue Letter Bible.org   Lexicon :: Strong's G746 – archē*
http://www.blueletterbible.org/lang/lexicon/lexicon.cfm?Strongs=G746&t=KJV

[12] *Powers – Blue Letter Bible.org   Lexicon :: Strong's G1849 – exousia*
http://www.blueletterbible.org/lang/lexicon/lexicon.cfm?Strongs=G1849&t=KJV

[13] *Spirit-Filled Life Bible by Thomas Nelson, Inc., Word Wealth page 1107*

[14] *Wisdom - Lexicon :: Strong's G4678 – Sophia*
http://www.blueletterbible.org/lang/lexicon/lexicon.cfm?Strongs=G4678&t=KJV

[15] *Doubting - Spirit-Filled Life Bible by Thomas Nelson, Inc., Word Wealth page 1646*

[16] *Tribulation – Spirit-Filled Life Bible by Thomas Nelson, Inc., Word Wealth page 1607*

[17] *Sift - Lexicon :: Strong's G4617 – siniazō*
http://www.blueletterbible.org/lang/lexicon/lexicon.cfm?Strongs=G4617&t=KJV

[18] *Place - Lexicon :: Strong's G5117 – topos*
http://www.blueletterbible.org/lang/lexicon/lexicon.cfm?Strongs=G5117&t=KJV

[19] *Joanna Weaver, Having a Mary Spirit: Allowing God to Change us from the Inside Out*

[20] *https://healethee.wordpress.com/2011/08/18/cnn-article-says-unforgiveness-anger-bitterness-can-ruin-your-health/*

[21] *Keep - Lexicon :: Strong's H5341 - natsar*

http://www.blueletterbible.org/lang/lexicon/lexicon.cfm?Strongs=H5341&t=KJV

22*Offense - Lexicon :: Strong's G4625 – skandalon*

http://www.blueletterbible.org/lang/lexicon/lexicon.cfm?Strongs=G4625&t=KJV

[23] *Take advantage of - Lexicon :: Strong's G4122 – pleonekteō*

http://www.blueletterbible.org/lang/lexicon/lexicon.cfm?Strongs=G4122&t=KJV

[24] *http://www.merriam-webster.com/dictionary/wiles*

[25] *Ensnare - Lexicon :: Strong's G2139 – euperistatos*

http://www.blueletterbible.org/lang/lexicon/lexicon.cfm?Strongs=G2139&t=KJV

[26] *Is drawn away - Lexicon :: Strong's G1828 – exelkō*

http://www.blueletterbible.org/lang/lexicon/lexicon.cfm?Strongs=G1828&t=KJV

[27] *Watch - Lexicon :: Strong's G1127 – grēgoreō*

http://www.blueletterbible.org/lang/lexicon/lexicon.cfm?Strongs=G1127&t=KJV

[28] *Wiles - Lexicon :: Strong's G3180 – methodeia*

http://www.blueletterbible.org/lang/lexicon/lexicon.cfm?Strongs=G3180&t=KJV

[29] *Righteousness - Lexicon :: Strong's G1343 – dikaiosynē*

http://www.blueletterbible.org/lang/lexicon/lexicon.cfm?Strongs=G1343&t=KJV

[30] *Justified - Spirit-Filled Life Bible by Thomas Nelson, Inc., Footnote page 1691*

[31] *Imputed - http://www.merriam-webster.com/dictionary/imputed*

[32] *Peace - Lexicon :: Strong's G1515 – eirēnē*

http://www.blueletterbible.org/lang/lexicon/lexicon.cfm?Strongs=G1515&t=KJV

[33] *Rule - Lexicon :: Strong's G1018 – brabeuō*

http://www.blueletterbible.org/lang/lexicon/lexicon.cfm?Strongs=G1018&t=KJV

[34] *Substance - Lexicon :: Strong's G5287 – hypostasis*

http://www.blueletterbible.org/lang/lexicon/lexicon.cfm?Strongs=G5827&t=KJV

[35] *Salvation - Spirit-Filled Life Bible by Thomas Nelson, Inc., Footnote page 1553*

[36] *Rhema - Spirit-Filled Life Bible by Thomas Nelson, Inc., Word Wealth page 1408*

[37] *Scripture - Spirit-Filled Life Bible by Thomas Nelson, Inc., Word Wealth page 1583*

[38] *Life - Lexicon :: Strong's G2222 – zōē* h

ttp://www.blueletterbible.org/lang/lexicon/lexicon.cfm?Strongs=G2222&t=KJV

Life - Spirit-Filled Life Bible by Thomas Nelson, Inc., Word Wealth page 1935

[39] *http://www.merriam-webster.com/dictionary/vigilant*

[40] *Vigilant - Lexicon :: Strong's G1127 – grēgoreō*

http://www.blueletterbible.org/lang/lexicon/lexicon.cfm?Strongs=G1127&t=KJV

[41] *Weary - Lexicon :: Strong's G5299 – hypōpiazō* h

ttp://www.blueletterbible.org/lang/lexicon/lexicon.cfm?Strongs=G5299&t=NKJV

[42] *Persist - http://www.merriam-webster.com/dictionary/persist*

[43] *Persistence - Spirit-Filled Life Bible by Thomas Nelson, Inc., Footnote page 1535*

[44] *Supplication - Spirit-Filled Life Bible by Thomas Nelson, Inc., Footnote page 1806*

[45] *Abundance - Spirit-Filled Life Bible by Thomas Nelson, Inc., Footnote page 1593*

[46] *The UBC Word for Today - http://ucb.cmhosts.net/index.cfm?itemid=88&testdate=09%20May%202002*

[47] *Sacrifice - Spirit-Filled Life Bible by Thomas Nelson, Inc., Kindom Dynamics page 1890*

[48] *Enthroned - Spirit-Filled Life Bible by Thomas Nelson, Inc., Kingdom Dynamics page 770*

[49] *God - Spirit-Filled Life Bible by Thomas Nelson, Inc., Word Wealth page 558*

[50] *Function of the Trinity - Spirit-Filled Life Bible by Thomas Nelson, Inc., Holy Spirit Gifts and Power by Paul Walker, page 2018*

[51] *Another - Spirit-Filled Life Bible by Thomas Nelson, Inc., Word Wealth page 1603*

[52] *Grieve - Lexicon :: Strong's G3076 – lypeō*
http://www.blueletterbible.org/lang/lexicon/lexicon.cfm?Strongs=G3076&t=KJV

[53] *Convict - http://www.merriam-webster.com/dictionary/convict*

[54] *Helper - Spirit-Filled Life Bible by Thomas Nelson, Inc., Word Wealth page 1605*

[55] *Sealed - Lexicon :: Strong's G4972 – sphragizō*
http://www.blueletterbible.org/lang/lexicon/lexicon.cfm?Strongs=G4972&t=KJV

[56] *Guarantee - Spirit-Filled Life Bible by Thomas Nelson, Inc., Word Wealth page 1753*

[57] *Tarry - Lexicon :: Strong's G2523 – kathizō*
http://www.blueletterbible.org/lang/lexicon/lexicon.cfm?Strongs=G2523&t=KJV

[58] *Spirit-Filled Life Bible by Thomas Nelson, Inc., Word Wealth page 1632*

[59] *Be filled - Spirit-Filled Life Bible by Thomas Nelson, Inc., Study note 5:18 page 1794*

[60] *Tongues - Lexicon :: Strong's G1100 – glōssa*
http://www.blueletterbible.org/lang/lexicon/lexicon.cfm?Strongs=G1100&t=KJV

[61] *Edifies - Lexicon :: Strong's G3618 – oikodomeō*
http://www.blueletterbible.org/lang/lexicon/lexicon.cfm?Strongs=G3618&t=KJV

[62] *Southern Baptists Change Policy on Speaking in Tongues -*
https://lastdaysnews4christians.wordpress.com/2015/05/16/southern-baptists-change-policy-on-speaking-in-tongues/

[63] *Boldness - Spirit-Filled Life Bible by Thomas Nelson, Inc., Word Wealth page 1632*

[64] *http://www.merriam-webster.com/dictionary/love*

[65] *Desire - Spirit-Filled Life Bible by Thomas Nelson, Inc., Word Wealth page 1740*

[66] *Fullness - Spirit-Filled Life Bible by Thomas Nelson, Inc., Word Wealth page 1792*

[67] *Page 159 – Deny - Lexicon :: Strong's G533 – aparneomai*
https://www.blueletterbible.org/lang/lexicon/lexicon.cfm?Strongs=G533&t=KJV

[68] *Sincere - Lexicon :: Strong's G505 – anypokritos*

https://www.blueletterbible.org/lang/lexicon/lexicon.cfm?Strongs=G505&t=KJV

[69] Fervently - Lexicon :: Strong's G1619 - ektenōshttps:

https//www.blueletterbible.org/lang/lexicon/lexicon.cfm?Strongs=G1619&t=KJV

[70] Pure - Spirit-Filled Life Bible by Thomas Nelson, Inc., Word Wealth page 1411

[71] Stronghold - Lexicon :: Strong's G3794 - ochyrōma

https://www.blueletterbible.org/lang/lexicon/lexicon.cfm?Strongs=G3794&t=NKJV

[72] Arguments - Lexicon :: Strong's G3053 – logismos

https://www.blueletterbible.org/lang/lexicon/lexicon.cfm?Strongs=G3053&t=NKJV

[73] Meditate - Lexicon :: Strong's H1897 – hagah

https://www.blueletterbible.org/lang/lexicon/lexicon.cfm?Strongs=H1897&t=KJV

[74] Sound Mind – Spirit-Filled Life Bible by Thomas Nelson, Inc., Word Wealth page 1853

[75] Peace – Spirit-Filled Life Bible by Thomas Nelson, Inc., Word Wealth page 1334

[76] Living - Lexicon :: Strong's G2198 – zaō

https://www.blueletterbible.org/lang/lexicon/lexicon.cfm?Strongs=G2198&t=KJV

[77] Powerful - Lexicon :: Strong's G1756 – energēs

https://www.blueletterbible.org/lang/lexicon/lexicon.cfm?Strongs=G1756&t=KJV

[78] Pneuma - Lexicon :: Strong's G4151 – pneuma

https://www.blueletterbible.org/lang/lexicon/lexicon.cfm?Strongs=G4151&t=KJV

[79] Corrupt - Lexicon :: Strong's G4550 – sapros

https://www.blueletterbible.org/lang/lexicon/lexicon.cfm?Strongs=G4550&t=KJV

[80] Taken - Lexicon :: Strong's H3920 – lakad

https://www.blueletterbible.org/lang/lexicon/lexicon.cfm?Strongs=H3920&t=KJV

[81] Blessed - Lexicon :: Strong's G2127 – eulogeō

https://www.blueletterbible.org/lang/lexicon/lexicon.cfm?Strongs=G2127&t=KJV

Sources

www.ingramcontent.com/pod-product-compliance
Lightning Source LLC
Chambersburg PA
CBHW062039090426
42740CB00016B/2962